I AM Sarah's Daughter

How to Get God's Attention In Your Marriage…

The Real Happily Ever After

By Dawne Kirkwood- Santi

ISBN-978-0-974-9927-0-9

Dedication

Lovingly dedicated to The God of Abraham and Sarah, whose
wisdom and knowledge guides relationships and builds real God-
intended "power couples", without whom this path would not have
been discovered.

Acknowledgements

I am deeply indebted to those who unconditionally love, support and pray for me. I also thank God for the powerful ministers and ministries that have moved in their gifting on my behalf with authority from the very throne room of God along with those that continue to inspire and impact my life. I thank God for the love and support of family and friends along with a host of amazing individuals placed in my life who are too many to name.

Foreword

Dawne Kirkwood-Santi - Evangelist, Author and Speaker. As God uses Dawne and her much lived life likened unto that of Esther, being brought forth from the pit to the palace, from little white shoes, fairy tale dreams, fear of failure, loss, pain, abuse and rejection to a life of faith, miracles, mercies, restoration, love, healing and blessings. Brought forth in a way that only God can. Dawne Kirkwood-Santi –Evangelist, Author and Speaker, takes you on a remarkable journey through the pages of this book. Prepare to be transformed through The Holy Spirit as God's word is brought forth with revelation, knowledge and understanding allowing your mind to be transformed by the renewing of God's words and biblical principles as He uses Dawne and her life of a testament to His faithfulness, goodness and glory. You are sure to prosper and be in health as your soul will surely prosper.

-Dr. Regina M. Morris, Touched by Faith Ministries International

Table of Contents

PREFACE

When I was a little girl I wanted to go to ONE place: "Happily Ever After!" I saw this place as not just a happy place but a peaceful place. I pictured it as a place where I would feel safe and loved. I desired to go to the ball in that beautiful dress. I desired to be chosen by the prince and to be given the glass slipper. I wanted "Happily Ever After" and everything that went with it.

I would sit and daydream about that love that lasts forever. I knew exactly how it would feel. I would imagine meeting the prince and having stars in my eyes. I'd imagine him sweeping me off of my feet and swinging me around in circles. I imagined that we would get along and we would never ever fight. I wanted the love that lasts forever and I didn't just want it for me, I wanted it for my parents as well.

Even though we went to church twice a week, memorized scripture and prayed, there was discord in our house. It made no sense. I prayed and asked God to make my parents get along. I begged God to fix my parent's marriage but instead they got a divorce. I was left confused but somewhat relieved, thinking that God did not care about marriages, so I turned to Walt Disney.

I knew that Mr. Disney cared about marriages because he would take the couples where I wanted to go, "Happily Ever After." I watched every fairy tale, Snow White, Cinderella, and I was determined to get to that destination. "Happily Ever After" was the goal.

As I grew up I realized that I was not the only woman trying to get to "Happily Ever After." I watched as women found the "prince", married him and did not live "Happily Ever After"; and I joined them. I watched blissful happiness turn to divorce but I couldn't understand why. I did not know what it took to get to the "Real Happily Ever After." I began to doubt that it was "real."

Like many women I had the butterflies and I couldn't wait for him to call. I would tell friends about this amazing man and then something happened after I would say "I do."

I went back to God and He told me that He wanted me to write a book, but He said, "You have to live it first." I knew that it would not feel good. I had no idea that He was going to show me how to get to "The Real Happily Ever After." God took all of my questions, frustrations and broken dreams and led me to Sarah. He began to show me that my focus was on the prince instead of on The King and He showed me that it was possible to live in "The REAL Happily Ever After"…... Now through this book He's showing you how.

Introducing Abram and Sarai

Abraham is among one of the most famous men of the Bible. Abraham's name is mentioned a total of 294 times according to one reference; while another quote states 312 times. Abraham was originally named Abram and then God changed his name to Abraham. What I found interesting and what made a profound impact on me was the fact that not only did God change Abram's name to Abraham but God also changed the name of his wife Sarai to Sarah. This struck me as important because Jacob's name was changed to Israel after his life-changing event of wrestling with an angel. However, there is no notation of Jacob's wives, Rachael or Leah or anyone connected to him by way of marriage having experienced a name change; and yet God not only changed Abraham's name but his wife Sarai as well. This phenomenon must not go unnoticed. It truly said something to me that while God had changed Abraham's name He did not have to change Sarai's name but God chose to change Sarai's name to Sarah showing a distinct honor.

Sarai was extraordinary in being set apart and given such a powerful distinction by God. The fact that Sarai had captured the attention of The Almighty God and caused Him to do what He had done for no other woman captured my attention. I wanted to know more about this powerful woman that got God to take notice of her along with her husband during a time that women were not given the same honor as men. This honor that Sarai received was the same as that of her husband making it appear equal yet, Sarai is noted as calling her husband "Lord" showing the highest respect toward him as well as showing complete humility in Spirt toward her husband. I wanted to know more about his powerful woman. I wanted to know what power Sarai possessed that drew God's attention and, just as important, I wanted to know how I could receive the same attention.

I'm not sure where I first came in contact with the term "power couple" but there's no doubt that it described Abram and Sarai. Abram and Sarai showed up after the flood and after the tower of Babel. I pictured a power couple as a couple with a strong background and with their lives in total order. They present a united front and they have all the things that most people want and consider part of being successful. They have a "perfect" marriage. Their finances are well managed. They have security, love, health, wealth and peace. This had to be the case of power couples, or so I thought.

Since the power couple is made of two both must be identified individually then as the whole so we can't take a look at Sarai without first looking at Abram...

Abram shows up in Genesis 11:26. "And Terah lived seventy years and fathered Abram, Nahor and Haran". Abram is born first of his father followed by Nahor and Haran, his brothers. This verse is prefaced by the back drop which lets us in on the family dynamics. Terah, is Abram's father who has Abram at seventy years old followed by his brothers Nahor and Haran. Haran had a son named Lot, we're told in verse 27, but Haran died before his father and in my Bible "before" is actually underlined to show how unusual it was for an adult child to die before the parent in that day and age. Lot is an orphan being raised by Terah, his grandfather and Abram, his uncle, according to verse 28. In verse 29 Sarah (Sarai) enters the picture. "And Abram and Nahor took them wives: the name of Abram's wife was Sarai." Verse 30 adds one of the strongest dynamics to the picture. "But Sarai was barren; she had no child."

Let's take a modern close to home look at what we just read. Sarai is single. She meets a man who is raising his nephew, in short, a single dad. Yes, the grandfather is helping but be sure she knows that if anything happens to Terah, Lot is going to be Abram's. She marries this man knowing he has a child, so to speak. That speaks quite highly of her character as so often, women who are single have stipulations that the man they marry cannot have any children. In this Sarai show's character, maybe it was compassion for Lot or maybe it was her desire for a husband or maybe she was willing to accept Abram with Lot as her total package with the hopes that she would fill their home with more children of their own. Let's note that there was no modern technology to tell Sarai ahead of time that she was barren, instead month after month after her wedding Sarai waited to become pregnant while her friends had babies. She then was referred to as barren. Imagine the depth of character and strength it would take to raise a child that was not yours while your own womb showed no sign of giving fruit. So often I realize that it's easy to miss valuable connections with people in the Bible if you just race through the verse; but if you stop and think of how you would feel in their position then their ability to overcome becomes your inspiration to do the same. When the individuals come off the page and become human in a way that each one of us can identify with their emotions individually, that sparks inspiration and makes the Bible real and valuable. Sarah is long overdue for such a look...

Verse 31 deals Sarai another blow… "And Terah took Abram his son, and Lot the son of Haran his son's son, Abram's wife and they went forth with them from Ur of the Chaldees, to go into the land of Canaan; and they came to Haran and dwelt there". So now in short Sarai has to move and leave her friends and family. Imagine the pressure and stress and the other waves of emotions that she must have experienced. How stressful is a move to you? How difficult is the unknown? Most of us before a move might visit the city and check out homes, or for those who don't we may get on the internet and look at the house, art districts, schools, and the other features that the town may offer. Sarai had none of these options. There was no internet to surf the web and check out houses or the social media or the phone. She just had to pack up and go. That puts things in a different perspective. Sarai's character continues to stand out. She takes on the move like the woman that she is and after the long journey she settles in. Sarai is hit with yet another blow, in verse 32, Terah, her father-in-law, dies. She now has to console her husband and her family just got smaller. Sarai is well aware that there is nothing that she can do to grow her family by having babies. Chapter 11 of Genesis closes sadly but Chapter 12 brings hope for Sarai.

God's First Conversation with Abram

"Now the Lord had said to Abram, Get you out of your country, and from your kindred, and from your father's house, to a land that I will show you; And I will make of you a great nation and I will bless you, and make your name great; and you shall be a blessing; And I will bless them that bless you and curse them that curses you; and in you shall all families of the earth be blessed." Genesis 12: 1-3. Finally great news for Sarai. God had his first conversation recorded with her husband. She must have been thrilled! Can you imagine?? Your husband comes home and says: "Babe! I just heard from God!" Maybe you're washing dishes or making the bed and your back is turned toward him and he sounds extremely excited or in shock and you finally turn around and see his face and he looks completely changed. You can't explain it but you know that he's telling you the truth. You sit down and ask him to tell you what God said again and again until it takes root in your own heart and mind. I believe that's what happened with Sarai.

She must have replayed what God said over and over again... and I joined her. I looked at what God said. First he gave instructions "Get you out of your country, and from your kindred, AND from your father's house to a land that I will show you; In other words, MOVE! MOVE AWAY! MOVE AWAY FROM YOUR FAMILY! MOVE AWAY FROM YOUR FATHERS HOUSE! AND ONLY I KNOW WHERE WE ARE GOING! The other rendition could be, "in order for me to bless you, I've got to remove you from everything that is familiar and or makes you feel comfortable or anything that you've been holding on to for too long outside of me. "

Step One was moving out of:

what was comfortable

what she knew

what felt good

what she could see

what she trusted... and

who she was used to confiding in.

It had to sound stressful and scary but verse 2 offered promise. Verse 2 was God's part. It was what God would do if they followed what he asked of them in verse 1 "Get you"… was their part. "And" was God's part. "And "I" will make of you a great nation, and I will bless you, and make your name great; and you shall be a blessing: And I will bless them that bless you and curse him that curses you; and in you shall all families of the earth be blessed." Imagine that! God's part offered so very much and it included Sarai! God said He would make of her husband a great nation and that meant babies! That meant lots of them! At some point Sarai must have noticed that God's part had two components. Verse 2 told what God was going to do specifically for Abram and Sarai but verse 3 referred to how God would deal with others because of Abram and Sarai, in other words how their lives would affect and or influence others.

"And I will bless them that bless you, and curse him that curses you: and in you shall all families of the earth be blessed". In verse 3 God offers His protection. How amazing that Abram and Sarai received all of this from God in the first conversation!

No wonder verse 4 begins with the word "So" or for that reason, "So Abram departed as the Lord had spoken to him: and Lot went with him: and, Abram was seventy and five years old when he departed out of Haran."

While Sarai was hopeful because of God's words, another move was facing her. Imagine you just moved and a year or two passes by, you've finally found a good place to fellowship, you've made new friends and then your husband gets a promotion. While you may welcome the promotion, attached to the promotion is a move which may not be readily welcomed. Take note that the Bible gives no notation of Sarai being asked her opinion or thoughts concerning the move. Instead it is depicted as God spoke and Terah and Abram made the decision and Sarai followed. There is one word that suggests this to be true both in the first and second move, the word "took". Gen. 11:31 says "And Terah took Abram his son... and Sarai". Gen. 12:5 uses the same word, "And Abram took Sarai his wife and Lot his brother's son and all their substance that they had gathered and the souls that they had gathered, in Haran, and they went forth to go into the land of Canaan; and into the land of Canaan they came". (Gen. 12:5)

There is recorded no argument from Sarai about the move instead a willing spirit is suggested. In my mind's eye, I can imagine tents coming down and being gathered, animals, sheep, goats and cows being herded along with donkeys and camels being watered and readied for the move. Children of servants being placed on mules as the caravan begins to move while Sarai carries the one and most important valuable, hope! Sarai now carries with her hope from the promise given to her by God through her husband. Sarai's promise and blessing was given by God to her husband but it was to come through her. I found this most interesting that God did not just skip Abram and tell Sarai first that she was going to have a child that would bring great nations. Instead, God spoke to Abram telling Abram his plans for Abram which included Sarai and Abram then told Sarai causing Sarai to not only trust God but also her husband! I believe that God did this for a reason. I believe God wanted to establish and confirm his order to create this power couple. I believe God was saying this is my order, I AM first, then man as head then the wife. I believe in so doing he was teaching us a valuable lesson.

Was God making Sarai a second class citizen? No, and as you continue to read you will see that God was giving Sarai power! You will see that Sarai was a powerful woman, because she embraced the order of God as well as the promise. Before we go any further, it is important that you see that in this first conversation with God where God tells Abram to move and promises blessings and protection God included you! Yes. You are included. That's why I wrote this book. I saw that God included me in this promise and he included you as well. The last part of verse 3 says, "and in you shall all families of the earth be blessed." (Gen. 12:3). If you are a family, on the earth then you are being promised a blessing through Abram and Sarai. I am aware that theological scholars reference Gal 3:8 concerning this passage but God showed me that while that is true there is more. There is another component that is simple and plain that will cause families of the earth to be blessed which comes through Sarai. This component though simple and plain is not received through flesh and is given by becoming Sarah's daughter. It is received through the study of her life and her character and the relationship that she had with God. This component, if received by you, will change your life and your marriage as it did mine. God gave Abram a promise which he shared with Sarai which if received will bless the families on the earth, my family and now yours.

Let's get back to Sarai and the move. In Gen. 12:5, Abram and Sarai are in Canaan. Verse 6 finds Abram passing through the land to the place of Sichem, to the plains of Moreh. "And the Canaanite was then in the Land." Gen. 12:6, Abram and Sarai were not passing through friendly territory, the opposite was true. The Bible stated that the Canaanites were in the land, meaning enemy. Sarai had to move and travel under difficult weather conditions. In short, it was hot during the day and cold at night. She was traveling with animals on her way to a place that she did not know, trusting that her husband had heard correctly, and going through enemy lines. Now that sounds stressful, yet thus far we hear no complaint from Sarai. In Verse 7 right after we are told that they are surrounded by the enemy, Canaanites, God shows up and speaks. "And the Lord appeared to Abram and said, "To your seed will I give this land: and there built he an altar to the Lord, who appeared to him." Loving Father, God appears to Abram to reassure him. God appears to Abram and tells him that he will give the Land to Abram's seed.

God's Second Conversation with Abram

God showed himself to Abram for the second conversation and again Sarai is not spoken to at that time by God but she is included in the promise. Is God teaching Sarai? Is he reinforcing once more His order? Is God empowering Sarai? God was teaching Sarai to trust Him and her husband along with teaching her to respect His established order. God was saying to Sarai I know the desire of your heart for a child, and I believe Sarai heard that through the words conveyed to her through her husband. Sarai was learning one of the most difficult lessons that wives who are her daughters must learn, to trust God and their husbands. By God showing up at the time when Sarai was following her husband's leadership right through enemy lines was God's way of saying, "Well done daughter. I know this is not easy but I see you following his (your husband's) lead as he is following me, even though you don't know where he is going." God appearing to Abram at that time was also for Sarai. The Bible does not state any words about her emotions at that time but we know as a woman there had to be a gamut. Sarai was a woman going through the desert. Did I mention snakes? They were threats in the desert. I saw a snake outside of my front door a few days ago and I can't begin to explain the scream. I hate snakes but I felt sorry for it after. It was apparent that my scream threw it into a panic and frenzy. It was almost as afraid as I was, and it was a small garter snake. Imagine the snakes in the desert! But Sarai was following God and her husband or should I say Sarai was following her husband; as he followed God.

Abram "built an altar to the Lord who appeared to him." Appeared to "him" not "her" or "them", Sari is not there when God appears. Sarai could have easily felt left out and jealous and upset. She could have easily said "Babe, the next time you see God tell Him that He needs to let me know where we are going, and is there a mall near by" or she could have become obstinate and stubborn and said "Okay, that's it! He came and spoke to you twice and didn't bother to even send an angel to talk to me? Honestly what's this? You tell God that I'm not moving until He shows himself to me as well!" How many of us would have said that? But Sarai was learning leadership skills. Leadership? Yes. True leaders must first learn to follow. Sarai heard the promise and she believed the promise but she grasped that God had established an order and she was walking in it. She was taking note of what was being done. Sarai was watching God. Reassurance was being given to Sarai by God her husband and she was receiving it in faith from him. How easy would it have been for God to have appeared to Abram and said, "I'm with you." That would have been reassuring in the midst of enemies in the desert but that message would not have touched on the desire of Sarai's heart. But God speaking to Abram the second time and using the word seed, He included Sarai. "Seed" meant children or at least one and grandchildren.

When I had a garden, I had no idea about planting. I planted several seeds of one thing like lettuce or in one case beets. I could not believe how many heads of lettuce came from one seed. The beets were so in abundance that I needed garbage bags to harvest them. I kept thinking how can you get so much from each seed but God is a generous father and he can bring a multitude from one seed. The word seed meant more abundance and generation and all of that would start with a child. God was speaking to Abram and giving hope to Sarai through Abram by using the word seed, letting Sarai know that He was not leaving her out. God was letting Sarai know that she was part of His plan to bless them and all of us as well. Once again God was establishing His order. Abram in gratitude built an altar, a place of worship to the Lord before he moved. Sarai was watching what worked. God was teaching Sarai a template. God had appeared to her husband. God included her in the message that came through her husband of blessing and her husband established an altar of worship before he moved. Sarai was paying attention as should we.

In verse 8 we find that Abram and Sarai are moving again. "And he removed from there to a mountain on the east of Bethel and pitched his tent, having Bethel on the west, and Hai on the east: and there he built an altar to the Lord, and called upon the name of the Lord." Sarai watched as Abram prayed, "called upon the name of the Lord" then moved after both building an altar and praying. Sarai was seeing a pattern of God speaking to her husband and giving instruction and hope and direction. Then she saw her husband follow the instruction. She saw that when the instruction led to seeming danger, God spoke to her husband again giving reassurance and hope. Sarai saw that after God spoke to her husband, her husband moved and she saw her husband initiate conversation with God after building an altar and she saw him build an altar after God spoke to him. She saw that her husband moved when God spoke and did not move until he spoke to God even when God did not speak. I'll repeat that. Sarai saw that her husband moved when God spoke and did not move unless he spoke to God even when God was silent.

24

When true communication is taking place only one person is speaking at a time. The other person is doing one thing, listening. When God was speaking, Abram was listening. If instruction was given he then followed it. When God was not speaking and Abram was not following instruction in that exact moment, Abram was initiating conversation with God. Note that Verse 8 states that Abram "called upon the name of the Lord" but there is no documented answer from the Lord. Maybe Abram just received a sense of quiet peace that God often gives His children but we see no documented conversation from God at that time but we do know that Abram did not move until he sought God. Sarai saw that her husband did not move until he initiated a conversation with God.

Verse 9 begins with "And" showing the connection to the last thing that he did. It suggests that when Abram called upon the name of the Lord in verse 8 that Abram was given direction or the peace to know that God did not change direction hence that was why God did not speak in such a way that warranted recording. Verse 9 says "And Abram journeyed going on "still" toward the South. The key words to know what took place in the prayer of Abram was his actions after the prayer in those two words "and" and "still". God was quiet because His direction had not changed. It's obvious that before the prayer Abram was going south and that is seen in the words "still". "And Abram journeyed going South still."

In Genesis 12:9 Sarai saw that God spoke when He had something to say. If God already gave instruction He didn't need to repeat Himself and when God does repeat it's for our benefit and reassurance. God's direction to go toward the south still stood. How often do we pray and God gives us an answer but we may not like it, so we pray again but God is silent. I have found in my life like with that of Abram and Sarai that it means that God has not changed direction or instruction so I have to go "still to the south". When my marriage was going through a difficult time and I was tempted to give up, God's word did not tell me to change directions. My marriage looked like it was "going south" to the human eye. We often say when something isn't going right that it "went south from there" but sometimes God says go south and the trial gets more difficult. It may make no sense, but that's when God gives us an opportunity to put into practice what we have learned. Sarai had been watching her husband and hearing God's words through her husband. She had heard all of the promises and she was going to have an opportunity to put what she was learning into practice. In verse 10 Sarai sees things "go south". "And there was a famine in the land". That was not great news. Verse 10 gives us a better look at Sarai's situation. "And there was a famine in the land: and Abram went down into Egypt to sojourn there; for the famine was grievous in the land." Abram decides to go to Egypt and sojourn because of the famine. What Sarai had to have noticed as I did, was that her husband did not establish an altar and or call upon the Lord, at least there is no documentation of such. It says there was a famine in the land and Abram went down into Egypt to "sojourn" there. The circumstance was famine and the decision, to go down into Egypt was made based on the circumstance. Because there was a famine Abram went down into Egypt. It suggests that had there been no famine, Egypt was not the place that Abram would have considered. Egypt was known to have many gods. It was not stated anywhere in my Bible that Abram was told to go down to Egypt.

Sarai was watching her husband's pattern of prayer and speaking to God and building an altar of worship before each move but she did not see that pattern this time. Instead Sarai saw that there was a bad circumstance and there was a move and a decision but she also saw that it was not prefaced by her husband's usual, hearing from God

27

then building an altar and "calling upon the name of the Lord." Sarai had to have been filled with that woman's intuition that we often feel when something is about to happen and it's not good but there is no conversation noted of Sarai pointing out "Babe, you've got all of us following you and you know I'll follow you anywhere "But" I didn't see you build an altar. I didn't see you pray." It must have been tempting since she must have noticed, yet she refrained from having that conversation with her husband. There was no "Honestly Babe are you serious? A famine?" There was no reminder of "there was plenty of food back home." Sarai took no opportunity to question her husband in a time that was difficult neither did she remind him of any shortcomings. Sarai was a wife and she was all in. Sarai was on team Abram, Sarai knew that partnership is not part time. Her woman's intuition combined with what she saw as the break in pattern had to be screaming that something is about to go wrong yet she was silent on the matter.

Verses 11-13 of chapter 12 unfold what she must have been sensing through this conversation with her husband. "And it came to pass, when he was come near to enter into Egypt that he said to Sarai his wife, Behold, now I know that you are a fair woman to look upon:

Therefore it shall come to pass, when the Egyptians shall see you that they shall say, This is his wife: and they will kill me, but save you alive. Say, I pray you, you are my sister: that it may be well with me for your sake; and my soul shall live because of you". Sarai truly was a wife! It would have taken everything I had, before God taught me the principles that I'm sharing with you, to have been quiet at this point had I been Sarai! I would have "gone in". There was no way I would not have said, "You want me to do what?" Sarai exhibited total restraint. She showed the ultimate respect for Abram. At this point Sarai could have easily said "Hold on Babe, okay first of all thanks for the compliment but you're talking crazy talk! Didn't you talk to God? Didn't He say that He was going to make nations out of you? Babe, how is that possible if he allows the Egyptians to kill you because of me? Abram, where is your faith? I'm your wife! Are you really asking me to bend the truth for you? And what about me? What if they do something to me?" But, no Sarai had seen too much.

Sarai saw that her blessings were coming through Abram and Abram's blessings were coming through God. She knew that God had established an order that He would speak to her husband. She believed that if she respected Abram that God would handle the situation. Sarai stayed in the order that God had set up. She saw that God could speak to her husband! She believed that God would handle the situation if she stayed in His order and if she stayed in respect and in obedience to Him even when it did not feel right at the time. This trait of Sarai's is one of the difficult ones to develop. Being a daughter of Sarai means studying this trait and the order that God had established and shared with Sarai. Sarai had listened to the things that her husband Abram told her that God had said to him. She realized that if what Abram had told her about God's promise to make him a nation was true, then God would not allow evil to happen to her since she was a part of God's plan. Even with this information, Sarai respected her husband's wishes and obeyed. Yes, I said obeyed. God rewards obedience. It is a key principle.

God also rewards following His order. Sarai knew that God was head of Abram and Abram was her head. She respected God's order and trusted that God would work things out in her favor as long as she did well. Sarai, though married to Abram, had to be counting on God. Think about it. Sarai knew that if Abram was correct, and the Egyptians saw her and wanted her and she said she was Abram's sister it was, in short, saying that she was available! By protecting Abram, she was placing herself right in harm's way! Sarai had to know by being obedient to her husband she would be jeopardizing what she cared about, her own safety. How many times do we as wives and women chose to disobey our husbands because we feel like if we disobey and step out of God's order that we will get what we want when it's the complete opposite. I've found that when I stay in order, even when I totally disagree, and I talk to God, God will speak to my husband and ultimately, I get what I want. Sarai obeyed truly unto death since she had no idea if this act of obedience would lead to the death of her marriage or her own life. She had no idea if the Egyptians would take her and use her then disregard her. She had no one to insure her safety except God. Sarai decided to be obedient and trust God.

This would be a great time to insert the verse, "As a man thinketh, so is he". Exactly what Abram was thinking came to pass. "Life and death is in the power of the tongue". This must be true therefore it's good to remember to speak what we want to see come to pass. Verse 14 and15 give confirmation. "And it came to pass, that when Abram was come into Egypt, the Egyptians beheld the woman that she was very fair. The princes also of Pharaoh saw her and commended her before Pharaoh and the woman was taken into Pharaoh's house." Great, drama in Egypt! That did not take long! You may be wondering how they found themselves near the Pharaoh, who of course, was basically King? You and I can't just wander into the White House or anywhere close but if you are familiar with the story of Joseph we see that when there was a famine, people came from many places for food and it was distributed by Joseph for Pharaoh since he was appointed to do so. Genesis 41:34-35 shows the formula, "Let Pharaoh do this, and let him appoint officers over the land and take up the fifth part of the land of Egypt in the seven plenteous years. And let them gather all the food of those good years that came and lay up corn under the hand of Pharaoh and let them keep food in the cities."

While this is taking place in Genesis 41, after the time of Sarai, note that Joseph had interpreted a dream which told of how long the famine would be and the need for gathering and storing and building storehouses. It does not suggest that to be the first famine which obviously it was not as Sarai is experiencing a famine in Chapter 12 but it does suggest that the idea of storing and overseeing and distributing or selling grain to others during a famine was the template overseen by Pharaoh. Therefore, in order to get food in Egypt during a famine one must go through the Pharaoh.

Let's get back to Sarai. Sarai's been asked by her husband to say that she is his sister in order to save his life. Her husband Abram has told her that because of her beauty the Egyptians will want her and kill him to get her. Sarai knows that in obeying her husband, she places herself in a "God awkward" position, meaning one of those positions that you know it is awkward for everyone but God. Sarai obeys her husband, remains in God's order and trusts God. Abram's words and thoughts quickly manifest in verses 14 and 15 where Sarai is beheld as very "fair" interpreted as beautiful. She is commended, or complimented, by the princes of Pharaoh and taken into Pharaoh's house. Verse 16 finds Abram in a place where every wife would hope their man would say "Nah, man that's my wife, you can't have her. You'll have to kill me first." You know that part of the movie where the girl clutches her hands and looks at her man with puppy dog eyes and says breathlessly, "My hero." But Abram missed it. No such communication came out of his mouth.

If Sarai was holding her breath she could let it go. Sarai was on the auction block for her husband's protection and her obedience to her husband placed her there. She refused to step out of God's order even when it did not benefit her. How often, as a wife has your husband made a decision and you felt like you were "paying" for it, whether it was financially or emotionally? That's the most critical "I AM Sarah's daughter" moment. It is the time when the flesh wants to rise up and step out of the order. It's the time when I used to just say to myself: I am not going to stay on a ship where the captain doesn't see we are going to hit an iceberg. I'd want to take over! In fact, I would take over and the water would pour into the boat even faster. My problem was I saw my husband as the captain of the ship instead of God. It's easy during those times to abandon ship but changing husband's does not change you. It just changes your last name.

This was a great time for Sarai to abandon ship. Sarai could have said, "Honestly, I could use a good "come up" right about now! This man has had me moving from pillar to post literally! He's got no idea where he's going. I've moved how many times now? And if that's not enough he has me saying I'm his sister so I can protect him when he knows that he is supposed to protect me. My nails are a mess and all of this traveling is bad on my feet not to mention my hair! Look at the women in Egypt. They look amazing - beautiful bronzed skin. Their hair looks beautiful. And those princes don't look bad. I could get used to this and it would serve Abram right for the way he's treating me". We've all had our version of what could have been Sarai's conversation but Sarai was steadfast in her obedience to her husband and God's order. It didn't seem to be getting her anywhere. She was being taken from her husband while her husband on the other hand seemed to be gaining.

Verse 16 of chapter 12 states "And he entreated Abram well for her sake: and he had sheep, and he asses, and menservants, and maidservants and she asses, and camels." So, let me get this right; Abram is straight chilling while his wife is gone! Abram is being waited on hand and foot-literally. "Menservants and maidservants", other women are being brought to him to wait on him hand and foot! "Other women", surely Sarai will lose it now! Positively when she sees that her husband is not protecting her but prospering from the situation she steps out of order. But no, not Sarai. Sarai is committed to obeying her husband and staying in the order that God established and she is trusting God. But where is it getting her? You may say it's not fair. Here's what I've learned. God is not fair. What? I'll write it again. God is not fair. God is just. Think about it. Three women carry a baby and all of them give birth. One gives birth to a child that can't see, one gives birth to a child that can't hear and one gives birth to a child that's totally healthy and "normal". Is that fair? Furthermore a hundred more women will carry babies for nine months and all of them deliver healthy "normal" babies and is that fair? It becomes less "Fair" when you are the one with the child that's blind or deaf. God is not fair. God is just.

I had two healthy babies followed by one who had half of her small intestines removed when she was four hours old. I was so upset, I kept thinking "It's not fair." We were in New York at the time and had an opportunity to meet a young man and shared a Bible study with him. I recently found out that he now has a huge ministry teaching about the sanctuary, Ivor Meyers. God used that time in New York during that child's darkest hour to plant seeds and shed light. That baby is now a young woman.

So often we get caught up in what's "fair". We want our marriages to be "fair". "Fair" can be keeping you from being happy. Fair is always based on a comparison. They have two scoops of ice cream and I only have one. Have you ever wondered why it's called a "Fairy" tale? The fairy usually shows up to "even" out the board. She usually makes things "fair", equitable, making sure things are even. God isn't fair but I've found that he's just. God used that daughter being in the hospital to save so many individuals. He used it to build my faith; he used it to bring remarkable people into my life. He used it to teach me that He doesn't bless us based on what he's doing for our neighbor. He doesn't bless or distribute based on comparison. He used it to teach me that He is just. Just to me means if I could see the end of it I'd say "okay God leave it "Just" the way it is." Sarai was not stepping out of "just" to get "fair". FAIR is how man looks at things. Just is how God looks at things. "Fair" places our eyes on the other person in the situation. "Just" places our eyes on God. Sarai had every reason to say that's not fair. She could have looked at what her husband was doing but Sarai committed to be obedient to her husband and trust God. Sarai committed to keep her eyes off of her husband so she would not fall into comparing and instead Sarai committed to keeping her eyes on

37

God. Sarai was in a situation where her husband had selected his way of thinking and she was bearing the consequence.

Sarai knew that her husband could have selected to operate differently, maybe more honorable and more honest in her eyes but she also knew that her husband's behavior did not dictate hers. Sarai committed her head to obeying her husband and staying in the order that God established and Sarai chose to trust God. Sarai had to know that if she was obedient when her earthly husband didn't step up, her Heavenly Husband would. Sarai was standing on the template being obedient to her husband and trusting God. Sarai was going to respect her husband, stand in her appointed place, despite what was "fair", or "not fair". Sarai was trusting God. Her husband did not protect her. She could not protect herself in any other way besides obeying. Sarai recognized that obedience is protection. Sarai realized that if she did not "break rank", she was protected. In the military, there is a chain of command. Each person is to report to their immediate supervisor. If you do not get satisfaction from that supervisor, you are allowed to go up the chain of command until you get the satisfactory answer. Sarai did not break the chain of command. Sarai followed the instructions of her husband and did

38

not allow her opinion or her emotions or her companion's opinions to keep her from obeying her husband.

Sarai knew that Abram, her husband, was her head and above her. She knew that God was Abram's head and above him. Sarai knew like those in the military that you have to follow the orders given by your immediate supervisor in order to have action taken by that person's supervisor. Sarai knew that she had to follow Abram's instruction in order to get God, Abram's head, to step in for her. Sarai understood headship. Sarai followed the command of her headship allowing his (Abram's) headship to step in and take over. Thank God for verse 17 "And the Lord, plagued Pharaoh and his house with great plagues because of Sarai, Abram's wife". I had to shout hallelujah. This verse changed my life and my marriage! I kid you not! I had to shout hallelujah. "And The Lord," we can just stop there! Not "and Abram", not "and her servants and her friends", it said "And the Lord". Let me break that down. "And the inventor of the eyeball that is reading this right now transmitting messages to the brain to interpret it", "And the one who hung the stars in place", "And the Ancient of Days", and "The Alpha and Omega", and "The I AM that I AM" stepped into Sarai's situation because she was obedient! I can't stop crying right now because so many of you are going to get this like I did. Read it again and again until you do.

Sarai got God's attention and her obedience moved the hand of God and Sarai didn't say a word! I'm crying right now because becoming Sarah's daughter got me everything that I wanted from my husband. I just stopped asking him and remained in God's order. The Holy Ghost told me: "Be quiet. Let me speak for you". "I AM Sarah's daughter" changed me. It changed my focus. It changed my marriage and it changed my life. Now, it can change your life, your focus and your marriage. If you aren't married yet becoming Sarah's daughter will change what you look for in a marriage.

Abram was not perfect but he was loved of God. Your husband isn't perfect but he too is loved of God. Let me remind you of something that I saw in Genesis 2:18 "And the Lord God said, It is not good that the man should be alone; I will make him a help meet for him". God had just made man. He had not sinned. He was in his perfect state when God said that it is not good that the man should be alone and He created a help meet for him. That means that man needs our help. We were made to help them. It is so tempting when they leave us or place us in situations like Sarai found herself, to leave them alone, but God said," it's not good that they be left alone and we are to help "meet", maybe help "meet" their goals, maybe help "meet" our own expectations of them!

When we go into anger it opens our hearts to become as stone. It leads us to rebellion and stubbornness, and it is hard and I mean hard, to get out of that state. I've been there! I'd be so angry and I had opened myself to such stubbornness and I could have conversations in my head telling myself how to approach him, telling myself what to say to get back, but the gap was getting bigger by the second. My pride was a little puppy that I was only feeding every now and then, but after an argument I'd turn around and Pride, the puppy, had grown into a Great Dane-Pit bull mix and it was bigger than me! I fully understood how the Bible says that rebellion and stubbornness is the sin of witchcraft. "For rebellion is as the sin of witchcraft, and stubbornness is as iniquity and idolatry" 1Samuel 15:23. Once I was angry another spirit took over. I was no longer in control. It took me quite some time to really understand this but being stubborn leads to a spirit other than God's, making the heart hard. Anger at my husband caused a gap inside of me. Every time I I felt anger toward my husband I would, in my head, take back my heart. I would say to myself, "He obviously cannot protect my heart. He's breaking it so I have to take it back". When I became Sarai's daughter I realized that my heart is not his to protect. I realized that it's God's job to protect my heart and I'm trusting God to share my heart with my husband. I trusted God to keep my heart safe and to "sit down" in my marriage.

Some of you may understand that you can't protect your own heart and love at the same time. Every time I "took" my heart back in my mind, in my spirit it created a physical shift in the wrong direction. Everything that takes place in the seen must first take place in the unseen. My thoughts were not seen but they were affecting and creating those things in the physical world. The act of moving my heart was causing things to become even worse in my marriage. The more I tried to protect my own heart the more it would hurt. It seemed to cause my husband to become more difficult toward me in whatever situation that we were facing and he didn't even "know" (or so I thought) that I was moving my heart so I could protect it. I never announced that I was not "sitting" in my marriage at those times of anger but it could be felt.

When we get married we "sit" rather comfortably in our marriage. It means we unpack, get comfortable, we say basically that we aren't going anywhere and that's what I did. With each disagreement that I handled with anger, even when I didn't show it on the outside, caused me to move up a little in my "seat" and then eventually I began to "stand" up in marriage inside. If you're at your girlfriend's house and you're all laughing and talking, when you decide to leave the first thing that you have to do is to stand. The same thing is true in a relationship and I don't mean physically. I mean emotionally or spiritually or both. We all know women "leave" way before we leave. The physical act of leaving is usually the very last thing a woman does. So, instead of "sitting" in my marriage when I would get angry I was "Standing." Standing includes "leaving the man alone." "And the Lord God said, It is not good for the man to be alone; I will make a help meet for him" (Gen. 2:18). In my head once I began "standing" I was leaving the man alone and even though I was doing this "only in my mind", it was keeping me from the very things that I wanted in my marriage. Why? Because "as a man or woman thinketh so is she" (Prov 23:7). Every time my expectations of my marriage weren't met and I chose to protect my heart, make a shift, move out of my seat, "stand" up and move to "leave the man alone," things got worse! I began to pay attention. I

43

was getting what I didn't want plus I was exhausted! Thank God for the Holy Ghost! God in His mercy began to teach me to "sit" down and remain planted in my marriage. I didn't "sit" down because my marriage changed. My marriage changed because I "sat" down and decided to allow God to teach me and I gave him my heart and my marriage. I handed over my husband to Him as well, mentally, and I decided that nothing that I had tried was working so I'd try it God's way.

I began to get up early in the morning to talk about my marriage to God. I would wake up in the middle of the night and pray for my husband while he was fast asleep. I embraced being Sarah's daughter. I would tell myself I AM Sarah's daughter. I AM staying in God's order. God is first. My husband is headed by God whether he knows it or not and my husband is my head. Like Sarai, I AM will step into my situation as long as I walk in obedience to God and in obedience to my husband. I began to study God's word and the life of my "spiritual mother", Sarah. I saw Sarah not as just someone that I read about in the Bible. I began to identify with her and I could almost see her in Egypt in the Pharaoh's house. With strange men admiring her while her husband Abram was being attended by maidservants and I saw how difficult her decision to stay in God's order had to be, but I was sold.

Now where did we leave off in our story? Ah, yes… Sarai was in the Pharaoh's house separated from her husband seemingly unprotected while her husband was prospering at her expense, on the auction block so to speak, in verse 16. Things weren't looking good, but Sarai was staying the course, staying in God's order and trusting God while obeying her husband and in verse 17 things changed! "And The Lord plagued Pharaoh and his house with great plagues because of Sarai, Abram's wife!" (Gen. 12:17). Sarai not only received God's attention; Sarai received God's protection. Please note that the Bible says, "The Lord plagued, Pharaoh and his house because of Sarai, Abram's wife." It did not say that God plagued Pharaoh and his house because of Abram! God honored Sarai for honoring her husband despite his decision and God, not Abram, delivered her. God didn't just show up for Sarai but the Bible says that God "plagued Pharaoh and his house with great plagues" (Gen. 12:17). God made it clear that Sarai was greatly protected! God made it clear that He was not going to let anything happen to Sarai! God also made it clear that Sarai was a powerful woman! Sarai's commitment to her obedience moved the Hand of God and she had convinced me that I needed that kind of power. Sarai, through the pages of the Bible, had convinced me that I needed to become her daughter. What's really funny is that I would always say, ever since I can remember, that if I'm related to any person in the Bible it was to Abraham because I have crazy faith. I truly saw myself as Abraham's daughter but now I saw that I was being called not only to become Sarah's daughter but to call all of Sarah's daughters around the world to step forward and claim the blessings of being her daughter and allowing God to fight for our families and for us through obedience to God.

Once I said, "I am Sarah's Daughter" it became my mantra. I began to picture her situation and disposition while in Pharaoh's house. I pictured Sarai remembering her husband making an altar to the Lord and "calling upon the name of the Lord". Gen. 12:8. Even though the Bible gives no documentation of Sarai's prayer, I'm sure she called upon the name of the Lord. Maybe Sarai sat in the deep tubs in the house of the Pharaoh and enjoyed the mud baths and massages with warm oils with resolved confidence that God would show up. Maybe she was like me, witnessing to the maidservants who gave her the foot rubs, telling them about how the only true and living God appeared to her husband and that she knows that God is going to get her out of Pharaoh's house because He's powerful. In either case we know that God, The Lord, plagued Pharaoh and his house because of Sarai, Abram's wife. I love how the Bible states her name and her position, "Sarai, Abram's wife". Abram's wife was her title, and God not only honored but defended and protected her title.

Heavy-weight champions fight to get their title and then when they receive it they fight to keep it. Think about how hard it was for you to become your husband's girlfriend then how much you went through to finally get engaged. I couldn't wait for the title "fiancé". I really couldn't wait for the title "wife"! I couldn't wait for people to call me "Mrs". I wanted the title but I truly had no expectation that I would have to fight to keep it. Not only that but I didn't think that I "should" have to fight to keep my title. To make matters worse thoughts of giving up the title came too easily when trouble arose. How much respect would we have for Muhamad Ali if he won one belt and then got in the ring when someone challenged the belt and he did not throw one punch to defend it? How much respect would we have for Mike Tyson if he became the heavy-weight champion of the world but did nothing to protect or defend his title? Which boxer is given a belt to keep forever? Not a single one! You get the belt as long as you can beat those who try to take it. Yet I see the title of "Mrs." being handed over to the enemy without a fight! Sarai fought for her marriage through obedience to her husband. Sarai refused to just give up her title as wife. What about you? She was denied by her husband when Abram said "she is not my wife". She was abandoned publicly. Everyone that she was traveling with knew her business. The people that she was traveling with knew there was "trouble in paradise". Sarai could have thought "I'm done! If Abram wants to act like I'm not his wife then I'm going to act like he's not my husband! If he's going to deny me publicly then I'll deny him publicly." But Sarai was The Wife Champion of the World and she was not giving up her title.

Go Deeper... Get "I Am Sarah's Daughter, How To Get God's Attention In Your Marriage-The Workbook

Declaration of Wifelamation

I do hereby solemnly swear that I will fight for the title of WIFE on my knees. Which I received on _____ in the _____ year of Our Lord. I commit to fight in the spiritual to keep this title in Jesus Name. I commit to surround myself with those supportive of my title, a committed team in the corner. I commit to have and respect a "referee" to "ring the bell". I commit to cover my husband in prayer and having others that will commit to praying for us, without divulging our marital business. I commit to putting on the whole armor of God on my husband daily in prayer along with myself and my family. I commit not to just hand over my title without a spiritual fight in Jesus Name through the blood of Jesus. I commit to knowing that my husband is not my enemy because "we wrestle not against flesh and blood" (Ephesians 6:12). I commit to using these weapons. "For the weapons of our warfare are not carnal, but mighty through God to the pulling down of strongholds" (2 Corinthians 10:4).

Signature_____

_____

Accountability
Partner_____

Date_____

(Suggestion: Chose Another Sarah's Daughter as Accountability Partner)

Sarai could have operated like a "single" woman. Sarai could have operated in the "if he then me" mindset. We all know the "if he does that then I'll do this." That mindset turns our marriage and relationship into chess games. In a chess game, we make our moves based on the other person's moves. Sarai did not play chess with her marriage. Sarai did not base her moves on Abram's moves. In chess, you have to keep your eyes on the board to see what the other person is doing but Sarai kept her eyes on the order that God had established. Sarai took her eyes off of the board and placed her eyes on The Lord. People knew her business, eyes on The Lord. People seeing her publicly denied by her husband, eyes on The Lord. Husband is not protecting her, eyes on The Lord. Becoming Sarah's daughter isn't easy but I can promise you that it's worth it. Becoming Sarah's daughter isn't popular but once you become Sarah's daughter and you see like I did how your marriage can be radically changed, becoming Sarah's daughter will become popular because it works! And when women find something that works we tell everyone about it.

Sarah's daughters get God's attention. Sarah's daughters are powerful because they allow God to be their power! Sarah's daughters allow God to fight for them while they walk in obedience even when it doesn't look good.

Imagine, with me, Sarai in Pharaoh's house. She's been placed in a room and suite fit for a queen. She is being bathed in preparation to go into the Pharaoh. She's had milk baths and mud baths. Handmaids come into her room to bring her fresh delicacies courtesy of the Pharaoh, handmaids are waiting on her while she is waiting on

God. But on this day the Egyptian handmaids enter into her room with pimples - pimples on their faces, pimples on their feet, pimples on their hands. Sarai asks what is going on. One Egyptian handmaid explains, "She woke up like this." Another handmaid is heard screaming in the hall. She reports that all of the water in the house has turned to blood. Sarai hears yet more screams in the hall and another handmaid rushes in with the report that darkness has fallen on the house and Sarai's room is the only place that there is light. Yet another handmaid that worked in Pharaoh's kitchen reports frogs are in the ovens and others are screaming because locusts have covered Pharaoh's house. The handmaids calm down enough to notice that Sarai's bath water is still clean and clear. They notice that there is no blood in her water, no pimples on her skin, as a matter of fact, her skin is flawless. They notice that there is not one frog or locust in Sarai's room and somebody runs to tell the Pharaoh.

While the Bible does not give us the exact details of the plague that The Lord placed on Pharaoh and his house it most certainly states that the plagues were great. Please note that not only were they "great" but they were also plural that means He didn't just send one! If they were anything like the plagues that He sent to Egypt when He sent Moses to tell pharaoh to "let His people go"; there was a plague of insects, hail, boils, open sores on cattle, blood, locusts, darkness followed by the death of the first born (Exodus, Chapters 7-12). Sarai had stood for right in obeying God and now God, The Almighty, The "All Powerful" God was standing up for Sarai. Sarai's commitment to God's order and obedience to her husband moved God into action on her behalf without saying a word! God was plaguing Pharaoh's house "because of Sarai, Abram's wife." (Gen. 12:17). Sarai had to have been humbled by this profound act of love and protection on her behalf. It must have erased all of her abandonment issues, her issues of not being good enough. It must have soothed all of her questions about her purpose and it must have washed away any feelings of low self-esteem. It must have confirmed to her His undying love for her. It had to make up for the embarrassment of her servants and even Lot (knowing that she was asked to say that she was not Abrams wife but his sister.) It must have humbled her and placed her in total awe of God that "He", God, would do that for her.

When I was pregnant with my son I attended the concert of Pastor Whitley Phipps, a world- renowned gospel singer and preacher. I was sitting in the concert when he sang a song about God believing in my dreams. It moved me to tears. I knew I had to speak to him. I went to the lobby and tried to get an audience with him but was unsuccessful. I prayed that God would help me and a girlfriend came and asked me what was wrong. I told her I needed to speak to Pastor Whitley Phipps and she said she knew him. She sent a note with security and the next thing I knew Pastor Phipps walked over to us and gave her a big hug. She then told him that I was her best friend and he was to talk to me and encourage me. I had just rededicated my life to God and had no idea where my writing fit into God's plans. He told me the following story and then said to "write again, God will open the doors". Pastor Wintley Phipps met Oprah before she became famous. He shared that when he met her she was concerned about losing her job and he prayed for her. During the prayer, The Lord told Pastor Phipps that God was going to use Oprah to reach millions. When Pastor Phipps told Oprah what God shared with him her response was, "Do you really think he would do that for me?" Her response was one of total humility. Her response was one of someone who was hoping that God would move for her but was not sure. Her response touched my heart. We know now that God did that for her and more.

Sarai had to feel such love that it was overwhelming. Verse 18 places us at the next "And", "And Pharaoh called Abram and said, "What is this that you have done to me? Why did you not tell me that she was your wife?" I love it! Pharaoh knew that his house had been turned upside down and he called Abram! Notice that Pharaoh did not call Sarai even though Sarai was in his house! Why? Because Pharaoh was following God's order as well! Because Sarai stayed in God's order there was no blame given to her. Sarai's obedience in staying in order protected her from responsibility of blame but Pharaoh was probably so afraid to say anything to her because she was obviously prized of God! Pharaoh placed the responsibility right where it belonged with Abram, Sarai's head and husband.

The headship is shown in Gen. 3:9 "But the Lord called unto Adam." In the beginning when Eve sins, God goes straight to Adam to question him. Similarly, Pharaoh knew God's order and questioned Abram. In verse 19 the questions continue, "Why said you, she is my sister? so I might have taken her to wife; now therefore behold your wife take her and go your way." Did you notice that Pharaoh did not even give Abram a chance to answer? Abram did not say a word and I can only imagine Abram's face when they called him (Gen. 12:18). He was probably giving Sarai that look like what did you do? What did you say? Imagine his surprise when the Pharaoh did not threaten to kill him or his people. Can you imagine how he had to have been holding his breath on his way to see Pharaoh? It may not have been a surprise to him.

Imagine the guards of Pharaoh's house having pimples, on their faces when they went to get Abram. Imagine the driver of the chariot being covered in pimples as well. Imagine that it does not take long for everyone to realize that the only people who have avoided the plagues is Sarai in Pharaoh's house. The guards and chariot men are angry when they go to get Abram. Imagine that Abram sees the pimples on the guards and chariot's men. Imagine that he walks through the halls of Pharaoh's house being escorted by guards that he notices frogs everywhere and that he can barely see for the flies and locusts. Imagine that Abram begins to figure out that what he sees must be at the hand of God. Imagine all of his thoughts being confirmed by Pharaoh's question, "What is this that you have done to me? Why did you not tell me that she was your wife?" Imagine the gravity of conviction that Abram must have felt when he realized that not only did his decision affect Pharaoh but the entire house of Pharaoh. Imagine handmaids holding their babies covered with pimples. Imagine Abram's recognition that his decision did not just affect his wife but others as well.

How many times have you been in a situation in your marriage where your husband makes a decision that you may feel is the wrong decision and it affects not only your husband and yourself but also your children? Were you Sarai's daughter in those situations? Wasn't that Sarai's plight? Had her husband's decision affected her and others who were innocent? Did the entire house of Pharaoh have anything to do with Abram's decision? Again God shows that He recognizes headship. Pharaoh's house was under Pharaoh therefore they were represented by Pharaoh. Verse 20 states, "And Pharaoh commanded his men concerning him; and they sent him away and his wife: and all that he had."

Chapter 13:1 opens with "And Abram went up out of Egypt: he and his wife, and all that he had, and Lot with him, into the south" Abram is back on course. As we can see he is going south again but one thing I found is missing. There is no "I told you so," from Sarai! As a matter of fact Sarai is recorded to have said nothing concerning the matter! Okay, wait let me get this straight. Sarai's husband throws her under the bus so to speak and does not protect her. The Almighty God steps in on her behalf because of her obedience and respect for her husband and commitment to God's order and sends "great" plagues on Pharaoh's house because of Sarai and God himself delivers. Sarai's spirit was not one of un-forgiveness – notice no apology from Abram is noted. Sarai does not even say "See Babe, seriously, that is a real act of God". Sarai's behavior in this situation is what being a daughter of Sarai is about.

This situation when Sarai allowed God to convict and correct her husband while she held her tongue made me realize the power of being Sarah's daughter. To be honored in such a powerful way by the Lord and after such a valiant delivery, to be filled with humility instead of pride, made me want to be Sarah's daughter. It is for this reason that "I AM Sarah's daughter" became my mantra because after seeing how God moved for Sarai. I knew I wasn't the only woman that needed God to move in such a powerful way for them. Once I submitted myself to the Lord and surrendered my will to Him concerning my marriage and fully accepted His order, I became Sarah's daughter and my marriage changed. Things that were incredibly difficult became simple and easy. Disagreements that would bring separation in spirit between my husband and myself for days got resolved in minutes! You may be reading this and thinking well, my situation is different. I agree all of us are given different situations in our marriages because we are all different people but one thing remains the same and that's our God and His principles.

God's power to reach your heart is the same as it is to reach mine. God's power to reach my husband's heart is the same as it is to reach yours. God has no boundaries except those that we place on Him. Let us remember that Abram was referred to as the Father of Faith. If Abram was the Father of Faith who would you call the Mother of Faith? It would stand to reason after looking at Sarai's character and commitment in these verses that Sarai was just that. It takes faith to stand in a situation which seemingly benefits you nothing in order to be in obedience to God and believe that God will protect you. It took faith for Sarai to obey her husband and wait and believe that God would deliver her from Pharaoh's house. It will take faith for you to believe that God will honor your obedience in your marriage in placing yourself in God's order: God, husband, wife. We cannot operate in God's order without faith. The flesh will want to say "no" and give reasons why going contrary to God's order is the way, but we must remember that the flesh wants two things, to feel good and to be "right." Being Sarah's daughter does not always "feel" good and being Sarah's daughter means letting go of being "right".

Being Sarah's daughter for me meant exchanging being right for being righteous, and I learned that God's hand is moved for the righteous.

Merriam-Webster defines righteous as "acting in accord with divine or moral law: free from guilt or sin, conforming to a high standard of morality or virtue." Righteous is referenced as being in connection with "divine law." Merriam-Webster defines divine as "of, relating to, or proceeding directly from, God." According to these definitions, in order to be righteous or in order to operate from divine law it must proceed or originate from God. Being righteous or the act of right-doing according to divine law comes from God. Sarai pleased God, so much so that, God acted powerfully on her behalf. Hebrews 11:6 tells us that, "Without faith it is impossible to please Him." So we now know that in order to please God we must have faith. In order to be Sarah's daughters we must have faith. Verse 6 continues with "For he that comes to God must believe that He is, and that He is a rewarder of them that diligently seek Him". Sarai had faith. Sarai believed that God is, and that He rewards them that diligently seeks Him. Sarah's daughters must believe the same.

You may be saying but, "I've tried". Can I share something with you? I watched a movie once that changed my thinking completely. In the movie, Amistad, an attorney played magnificently by Mathew McConaughey was fighting a case for Africans, who were captured and brought on a slave ship to America. The lawyer had fought the case and won in the lower court but it was referred to a higher court. The lawyer had the interpreter explain that they had won on one level but it was referred to a higher level and that he "tried". When the lawyer said the word "try," the interpreter stopped and the lawyer who was passionately explaining noticed and looked at the interpreter and asked "What? Why aren't you interpreting?" The interpreter said, "There is no word for "try" in their language. Either you do or you don't." That scene changed my life! I realized that dogs don't "try" to bark, they bark. Fish don't "try" to swim, they swim. Cats don't "try" to meow, they meow. Birds don't "try" to fly, they fly.

Only humans step into "try" mode. "Try" is immediately non-intentional. The word "try" gives an option to fail in its onset presentation. Before becoming Sarah's daughter, I was in a sense "trying" to stay married. The out was always available on the outset.

If it doesn't "work out" was a term that ran through my mind. It is a term that has become quite prevalent in reference to marriage. Sarai wasn't "hoping" that her marriage would work. Sarai was committed to her marriage working and the workings of her marriage. Sarah's daughters believe that God is a rewarder of those who "diligently seeks him". Merriam-Webster defines diligent as "characterized by steady, earnest and energetic effort: painstaking." "Steady" is defined as direct or sure in movement, unfaltering, firm in position; fixed showing little variation or fluctuation, not easily disturbed or upset. Steady nerves, constant in feeling, principle, purpose or attachment. Let's get back to what you may be saying "Dawne, I tried." My question is: who do you believe that God is? Do you believe that God is a rewarder of those who diligently seek Him? Have you been diligent? Have you been steady? Have you been earnest? Have you been energetic? Have you been sure in movement? Have you been unfaltering? Have you been fixed? Have you shown little variation? Have you been not easily disturbed or upset? Have you been constant in feeling (positively?) I know some of us can say we've been constant negatively. Have you been constant in principle? Have you been constant in purpose? Have you been constant in attachment? Have you been righteously doing all of these things in connection with divine flesh in faith depending on the "divine" to ring about your desired result? Have you been in truth Sarah's daughter?

God knows that I had to be taught to be Sarah's daughter because I was naturally Eve's daughter. My flesh tended toward going off on my own much like Eve. My flesh leaned toward the behavior of Eve. "Oh, it's all good Adam, I've got it. I'll be back or not." My flesh lent itself to going off in the garden and having a full conversation with a snake without even noticing that I was not where I was supposed to be which was at my husband's side. When I'm serving my flesh and giving into self I know that I'm not being Sarah's daughter instead I'm being the daughter of Eve. If we want to see God move in our marriages we've got to become Sarah's daughters. Gen. 13:1 places things in even greater perspective. "And Abram went up out of Egypt, he and his wife and all that he had, and Lot with him, into the south". I find it interesting that prior to this verse, each time Sarai is mentioned she is referred to as Sarai,

Abrams wife. Until this verse. In this verse it says clearly "And Abram went up out of Egypt, he and his wife" It shows that Sarai was established. Her title was set. There was no question to anyone who she was anymore or her value both to Abram and to God but it was God that established her position and her value. It was not her husband. How often as wives do we look to our husband to establish our worth and or our value or step outside of God's order to find it? Hmmm... Back to verse 1. We are told that Abram left Egypt, and went "into the south." We see that Abram went back to the south and while we see that he goes south there is no mention of the famine having come to an end. The lack of announcement of the end of the famine suggests that the detail and or circumstance was now no longer determining Abram's moves. Again, there is no conversation from Sarai that's noted of her saying, "Babe, are you seriously taking me back from where we just came? I knew we shouldn't have gone to Egypt!" Instead silence is what's recorded of Sarai. Verse 2 states, "And Abram was very rich in cattle, in silver, and in gold." Note that this is not noted going into Egypt. One could conclude that Abram's wealth was new and due to Sarai. We see in verse 3 that, "he went on his journeys from the south even to Bethel to the place where his tent had been at the beginning between Bethel and Hai. To the place which he had made there at the first:

63

and there Abram called on the name of the Lord." We see, hear that Abram not only went south but passed up the place where he had once been and went past that place to where he had last heard from The Lord, in short he had to retrace his steps.

This is where most wives drop the ball. This is where Sarai could easily, with all right and correctly so, pointed out her husband's flaws but not Sarai. Sarai was being taught that when you don't follow God's leading it takes longer to not only get where you're going but you have to go back to where you last heard God and it takes longer. Sarai was watching the lessons that God was teaching her through her husband. She saw the lost time she literally experienced traveling further herself with her husband through the dessert with him and yet exemplified no spirit of resentment, bitterness or un-forgiveness. Sarai was truly a powerful woman and she was beckoning me to become her daughter. Sarai had just seen The God of the Universe move on her behalf because she stayed in respect and order to her husband and she was not releasing that power. Sarai did not say a word. In the next several verses we learn a little more about Sarai by learning more about her husband and the circumstances.

Verse 5-8: "And Lot also, which went with Abram, had flocks, and herds and tents. And the land was not able to bear them, that they might dwell together: for their substance was great, so that they could not dwell together. And there was strife between the herdsmen of Abram's cattle and the herdsmen of Lot's cattle: and the Canaanite and the Perizzite dwelled there in the land. And Abram, said to Lot. Let there be no strife. I pray you between me and you, and between my herdsmen and your herdsmen: for we are brethren." (Gen. 13:5-8). So, we see from these verses that Abram is referred to as rich but then he is said to have substance that is great." Abram is wealthy. We also see that with the disagreement between Lot's herdsmen and his herdsmen Abram moves quickly to create peace, so Abram is also a peacemaker. We also see that the reason Abram gives in making peace is that he and Lot are "brethren". This shows that Abram is a family man, at least his connection with Lot was important to him. Verse 9-10 continued with Abram's solution "Is not the whole land before you? Separate yourself I pray you from me: if you take the left hand, then I will go to the right; or if you depart to the right hand, then I will go to the left." Abram shows himself to be a gentleman and offers Lot the first pick of the land even though he could have chosen first. Sarai must have marveled as she saw these qualities, in her husband. "And Lot lifted up his eyes and behold all the plain of Jordan that was well watered everywhere, before the Lord destroyed Sodom and Gomorrah, even us the garden of the Lord, like the land of Egypt, as you come to Zora. Then, Lot chose him all the plain of Jordan and Lot journeyed east: and they separated themselves the one from the other." (Gen. 13:10-11).

Sarai has just experienced another move along with another loss. Yet we see no documented complaint, in addition Sarai could have been complaining to her husband, "Babe, he took the best land!" or questioning," Why did you let him chose first?" Instead we move quickly into verse 12 that described the environment, "Abram dwelled in the land of Canaan and Lot dwelled in the cities of the plain, and pitched his tent, towards Sodom. But the men of Sodom were wicked and sinners before The Lord exceedingly" (Gen. 13:12-13). Verse 13 has nothing good to say! One would think that it would be enough to say someone is wicked but not so, it states that the "men of Sodom were wicked and sinners before the Lord" topped off with the word "exceedingly". What does God do after such a description? He shows up.

God's Third Conversation with Abram

Sarai watches as God shows up for the third conversation in verse 14. "And the Lord said to Abram, after that Lot was separated from him, 'Lift up now your eyes, and look from the place where you are northward and southward, and eastward, and westward: For all the land which you see, to you will I give it, and to your seed forever. And I will make your seed as the dust of the earth, then shall your seed be numbered. Arise, walk through the land in the length of it and in the breath of it; for I will give it to you." (Gen. 13:14-17). Sarah Sarai watches for the third time as God speaks to her husband. Because of her supernatural delivery out of Egypt she must be paying even closer attention to what God is saying to her through her husband. Sarah Sarai mutters no more murmurings that suggest, "Wow again? This is the third time that you did not speak to me," instead Sarah Sarai must have gone over the message from the Lord numerous times in her head. She, like myself, must have noticed that God started the message with a command. "Lift up now your eyes and look from the place where you are northward, and southward and eastward, and westward" (Gen. 13:14) Sarai must have noticed that the command had a <u>timeframe</u> in which to carry it out, "now".

And a <u>location</u>, "northward, southward, eastward and westward". Sarai was seeing that God was being very specific. Sarai had to have noticed that the Lord began first with a command then with a promise, "For all of the land that you see, to you will I give it, and to your seed forever. And I will make your seed as the dust of the earth: so that if a man can number the dust of the earth, then your seed will be numbered".

Sarai noticed that the command was to her husband but she also must have noticed that she was included once again in the promise. She must have noticed that The Lord was once again giving her words of encouragement and promise through her husband. Sarai's heart must have been racing with hope. Sarai must have noticed that the Lord closed his third conversation with her husband with a command, "Arise, walk through the land in the length of it and in the breath of it." but sealed it with his word and promise, "for I will give it to you". (Gen. 13:17) Imagine the thing that you desire most and The Lord actually shows up and tells her husband that he is going to give it to you! What joy! Sarai is seeing the Lord teaching her through her husband and bringing words of encouragement through her husband. Sarai's commitment to God's order is solid and she's hopeful. Sarai watches her husband go back to his template in Verse 18, "And Abram removed his tent and came and dwelt in the plane of Mamre, which is in Hebron, and built there an altar to the Lord. Sarai must have been thinking, "Yes! My husband is back on track," One thing we know is, if she thought it, she certainly did not say it! Sarai's husband is back on track she must have thought, "Great, now I can relax," but the beginning of chapter 14 brings drama!

The leading characters in this drama are reigning kings.

There are Four Kings introduced in verse 1:

King Amraphel of Shinar

King Arioch of Ellasar

King Chedorlaomer of Elam

King Tidal of nations

In verse 2 we find those Four Kings made war against these Five Kings:

King Bera of Sodom

King Birsha of Gomorrah

King Shinab of Admah

King Shemeber of Zeboiim

King Zoar of Bela

Verse 3 tells us that war took place in the Vale of Siddim, known as the salt sea

Verse 4-7 leads us to believe that the last five kings lost the war and served ~~King~~ Chedorlaomer for 12 years and in year 13 they rebelled. In year 14 another war broke out. Chedorlaomer and kings that were with him fought:

Rephaim in a place called Ashteroth Karnaim

Zuzim in a place called Ham

Emin in Shaveh Kiriathaim

Horites in mount Seir unto El-paran near the wilderness.

When they returned they went to En-mishpat which is Kadesh and fought Amalekites and Amorites that dwelt in Hazezon-tamar.

A repeat of the same battle started again in verse 8. And there went out the king of Sodom and the king of Gomorrah and the king of Admah and king of Zeboiim and the king of Bela (Zoar) to joined battle with them in vale of Siddim. In verse 9, these 5 kings faced Chedorlaomer king of Elam, Tidal king of nations, Amraphel king of Shinar, and Arioch king of Ellasar. Verse 10 tells us "And the vale of Siddim was full of slime pits; and the kings of Sodom and Gomorrah fled and fell there; and they that remained fled to the mountain."

What does this have to do with Sarai? Now this is where it gets deep. Verse 11: "And they took all the goods of Sodom and Gomorrah and all their victuals and went their way." Basically there are four Kings, fighting five Kings for a second time, and it seems like just war. But that's until we get to verse 12 of Chapter 14. "And they took Lot, Abram's brother's son," it just got personal! In-law drama just got real for Sarai. "And they took Lot, Abram's brother's son, who was dwelling in Sodom, and his goods and departed. And there came one that had escaped and told Abram the Hebrew; (note that this is the first reference to Abram being Hebrew. Hebrews were known to have only one God, as opposed to their counterparts who had multiple Gods) for he dwelt in the plain of Mamre the Amorite, brother of Eshcol and brother of Aner; and these who were confederate with Abram." (Gen.14:13) Now in short Lot got kidnapped. This was definitely the perfect time to hear Sarai's voice, "See Babe, that's what Lot gets! He picked the better land plus he was totally disrespectful by not allowing you choose first." But Sarai is not noted to say a word. Verses 14-16 shares Abram's response to the kidnapping. "And when Abram heard that his brother was taken captive, he armed his trained servants, born in his house, 318 and pursued them to Dan. And he divided himself against them, he and his servants by night, and smote them, and pursued them to Hobah, which is on the left hand of Damascus. And he brought back all of the goods and also brought again his brother Lot and his goods, and the women also, and people."

Please note that Sarai did not object to her husband risking his life for his brother Lot. Abram shows himself to be quite valiant and courageous. Verse 17 gives a little more detail into what took place. Abram did not just go and get Lot and the women and people back, verse 17 says "and the king of Sodom went out to meet him after his return from the slaughter of Chedorlaomer and the kings that were with him at the valley of Shaveh, which is the king's dale." Abram

73

slaughtered all of the kings that were fighting against the king of Sodom. He wiped them out! Can we take a moment to truly take a look at Sarai now? Honestly, if you were in Sarai's place, what would you be thinking at that time? "Exactly!" "You raised up an army to go after your brother and you annihilated kings to go and get him and the women with him and you left me in Egypt in Pharaoh's house?" You know how something new happens and it makes you remember something old and it starts a "new kind of old that should have been said argument"? This was one of those perfect opportunities, Sarai could have continued with, "You put forth no valiant, courageous attempt, let alone effort, to get me, your own wife back?" She could have taken it even deeper, "That's because I'm barren." Sarai could have gone there and dropped some tears then ladies you know that she could have dropped the ultimate bomb, "You don't love me!" She could have done this complete with waterworks and we would all say rightfully so. Then Sarai could have concluded with the question followed by the blow. Sarai could have attacked with, "How am I supposed to respect you?" The justification question that says, because you didn't go fill in the blank I don't have to___ (fill in the blank). Sarai had every right to whine and protest, "You did all of this for Lot and he didn't even stick out his neck for you! I placed myself in harm's way for you. I

74

lied for you and you didn't raise a hand let alone an army to come and get me!" But Sarai had a true spirit of forgiveness so she carried no resentment, so she had no outburst.

When our husbands or fiancés do something that hurts incredibly and then they apologize, if we say okay or nod and go on to the next thing but in our soul and deepest being we have not forgiven them, then it begins to stew like, a slow pot cooking. It's like the almond milk that I place on the stove every morning. I make a Turmeric Chai drink that is amazing for the body. I warm almond milk and I place a teaspoon of Numi Chai latte for both myself and my husband each morning. I place it on the stove on the lowest setting while I get the vegetables out to make my husband's juices. Without fail, it seems like I'll look at the milk and it's barely hot, then there is no steam coming up on the milk, then I turn around and it's boiling over! That's exactly what happens with un-forgiveness. We place what the person has done to us on a low flame thinking that is tucked away but unfortunately as we continue to deal with our spouses or fiancés and we are harboring that wrong, the moment that they do something else and it doesn't have to be something big, the pot overflows and the outburst flies out. Out of nowhere we've lost it and said the very thing that we were trying to stuff. Why?

Because: un-forgiveness plus time = resentment

resentment + time = bitterness

bitterness + time = sickness

sickness + time = death

Sickness can be emotional, mental or physical. It can even be. "I'm so sick of_____ (Fill in the blank) concerning that person. (You're saying you need a longer blank;)

Here's the biggest secret ever revealed. You can't stuff anything and truly be healthy! You can't stuff conversations that needs to come out of you and have a healthy relationship. What am I saying? Should you have a conversation about everything that you are stuffing? Yes! With your husband? No! I'm not crazy! What I'm saying is to get those conversations out of you! That's where prayer comes in. Getting on my knees and telling God the things that bothered me and asking him to give me a true spirit of forgiveness was the answer for me. Crying out to my Heavenly Father to create in me a clean heart daily made the difference. I recognize that often we had to be tough to protect ourselves. We had to be hard to protect our hearts but you cannot love and protect your heart at the same time. I'll write that again: you cannot love and protect your own heart at the same time. What does that mean? It means that each time that you choose to protect your own heart, you are choosing not to trust and not to love. Remember that love means that you're trusting God to protect "your" heart while "you" protect the heart of your husband.

"The heart of her husband does safely trust in her." (Proverbs 31:11) That is not easy but that's what Sarai did and I am Sarah's daughter. Sarai was able to avoid the kind of conversations that I know that I definitely would have had with Abram before I became Sarah's daughter because Sarai canceled out the first equation of the formula. Sarai subtracted un-forgiveness so she could add time and have no resentment and add more time and have no sick relationship and add more time and experience no death in her marriage, so her formula equaled a healthy marriage.

Let's get back to Sarai. We find that in verse 18 of chapter 14 something amazing takes place. "And Melchizedek king of Salem brought forth bread and wine and he was the priest of the Most High God. And he blessed him and said, 'Blessed be Abram of the Most High God, possessor of heaven and earth, and blessed be the Most High God which delivered your enemies into your hand.'" (Gen. 14:18-20). What a blessing! Here is a king who is also a priest who recognizes what Abram is to God. He pronounces and confirms that Abram is blessed of the Most High God and that his actions were righteous in the sight of God and he also states clearly that God was with him and it was God that delivered Abram's enemies into his hand! What an honor for Abram but what a confirmation for Sarai! Can you imagine how she would have felt if she hadn't followed the formula and had a clean heart and "stayed tongue"? Imagine if she had lashed out and said the wrong thing! But Sarai was on the right side and in right action because her heart held no un-forgiveness. Verse 20 ends with Abram's action: "and he gave tithe to all."

Sarai was watching and learning "right" action. Sarai was learning from her husband that which pleased God. Sarai was learning what pleased God. I must say at this point that Abram gave "tithe." A tithe is 10% or a 10th of all that we have. Let me say that returning a faithful tithe, giving back 10% catapulted me forward like nothing that can be explained in the physical or natural. God bless the 90% left over to the point where I began to give more than the 10% just to see how it worked, and I don't have words! If you desire more not just financially but in every area of your life, give back the 10th or 10%. There is something in the 10th in trusting God to meet the need and most importantly there is something in the obedience. What if your husband does not believe in tithing? Respect him. Stay in order and tithe out of your personal money. God will honor that gift. A testimony beats a lecture any day. You may ask what to do if you have no money, then tithe your gifts or talents. Commit to give of yourself outside of your home in a way that does not benefit you and watch God bless! This may mean 10% of your day may be used helping a single mom pick up her children so that she can finish a shift at work. You can tithe by helping an elderly neighbor by running to the store and doing the grocery shopping for them. Tithing your time can mean volunteering to clean the church or the home of a new mom.

When I was in Wisconsin I had the awesome opportunity to fellowship with a group of Mennonite women. I learned that it was their custom to cook food for two weeks for each of the expecting mothers when they have a baby. I thought that this was the most practical expression of love and thoughtfulness, probably because I've been there five times and the last thing that I cared to do after having a baby was to cook. The ways of giving back through tithing your time are endless. Once tithing is done with a great spirit, a willing and cheerful spirit, blessings will follow.

Sarai was learning the things that please God by watching her husband. Sarai saw that her husband was a man of valor. Sarai saw that Abram served a God of valor. Sarai saw that Abram was courageous. Sarai also saw that Abram served a courageous God. Sarai saw that Abram was a conqueror. Sarai saw that Abram served a God that was a conqueror. Sarai saw that her husband was known by the king (of Sodom). Sarai saw that Abram served the King of Kings and was known by the King of Kings. In verses 21-24 Sarai saw that her husband was honorable in that he refused to take a bribe from the King of Sodom. Sarai saw that not only did Abram refuse to take a bribe, Abram refused to allow anyone to get or take God's glory for making Abram rich! "And Abram said to the king I have lifted up my hand to the Lord, the Most High God, the possessor of heaven and earth. That I will not take from a thread to a shoe lace, and that I will not take anything that is yours least you should say, I have made Abram rich." Gen. 14:22-23). Sarai saw that Abram was protective of God's glory. Sarai knew that Abram served a God that was protective of His own glory. We can confirm this in Isaiah 48:11 "For my own sake even my own sake will I do it: for how should my name be polluted and I will not give my glory to another." Isaiah 42:8 further confirms, "I am the Lord that is my name; and my glory will I not give to another, neither my praises to graven images."

Sarai was seeing her husband's character and Sarai was seeing the character of God in her husband's character! Abram was teaching Sarai the ways of God. Sarai was learning the ways of God from her husband. Sarai saw that Abram was concerned about the glory of God. Sarai saw that when Abram took concern in the things of God that God showed up! Look at chapter 15:1. It starts off with "After these things." After Abram shows his character of valor and courage, after Abram trusted God to deliver his enemies into his hands. After Abram received fame from the kings knowing his name, yet he gave honor to The Most High God. After the priest blessed and confirmed that he was blessed, after Abram gave tithes of all. After Abram lifted his hand to The Most High God, the possessor of heaven and earth, that he would not take "from a thread to a shoelace" or anything that belonged to the King. After Abram witnessed to the king, after Abram made sure the men that were with him took their portion (Gen. 14:24). After Abram dealt fairly with the men, his employees, and after Abram stood in integrity. After Abram made it clear that no man but God only would be allowed to take glory for making Abram rich - After all of these things, THEN "the word of the Lord came to Abram in a vision". After all of these things, God shows up to speak to Abram. Conversation number four takes place. "Fear not, Abram: I am your shield and exceeding great reward" (Gen. 15:1) God gives Abram a command. "Fear not". God then personalizes his visit by calling Abram by His name. - "I AM your shield and exceeding great reward." God promises not just a reward but a reward described by two adjectives: exceeding and great. The word Exceeding is defined as: very great, extremely, extraordinary, exceptional, to go beyond in quantity degree- rate, to go beyond the bounds or limits of, to surpass, be superior to, excel to be greater as quantity or degree. The word Great is defined as unusually large in size, by comparison. Unusual or considered.

"I Am Sarah's Daughter, How To Get God's Attention In Your Marriage-The Workbook

God's Fourth Conversation with Abram

Sarai saw that God showed up for Abram and now there was a fourth conversation with plenty of promise. Sarai must have listened intently as Abram shared with her what God had shared with him. Sarai too, must have played the words over and over in her head. "I AM your shield and exceeding great reward." Sarai saw that God was telling her not to be afraid and that God was her shield. A shield is defined as anything that provides protection or a guard, defense, cover, screen, security and/or shelter. If Sarai was a wordsmith and loved words like I do she must have thought of each definition and placed them altogether. Sarai like myself must have looked at what God was saying if every single definition was meant. If that was the case this is what Sarai would have heard,

"Fear NOT Sarai and _____ (Put your name in the promise, Sarah's Daughter)

I AM your shield.

I AM your protection.

I AM your guard.

I AM your defense.

I AM your cover.

I AM your screen.

I AM your security.

I AM your shelter.

And exceeding, very great, extreme, extraordinary, exceptional, beyond quantity or degree, beyond bounds or limits, surpassing superior, excelling to be greater as quantity or degree, unusually large in size by comparison reward, or what you will receive in exchange for your service or obedience!" Sarai had to have placed her own name in this promise and had to be blown away! Place your name in it and claim it for yourself. When I placed all of the definitions together I was blown away and humbled and honored.

Sarai had to be holding her breath as her husband shared the remaining contents of this fourth conversation. Sarai must have said "What else Babe? What else did He say?" But the fourth conversation was different.

"And Abram said, Lord God what will you give me, seeing I go childless, and the steward of my house is this Eliezer of Damascus?" (Gen. 15:2)

"And Abram said, Behold to me You have given no seed: and lo, one born in my house is my heir." (Gen. 15:3)

"And, behold, the word of the Lord came to him saying, "This shall not be your heir; but he that shall come forth out of your own bowels shall be your heir." (Gen. 15:4)

"And He brought him forth abroad and said, Look now towards heaven; and tell the stars if you will be able to number them: and He said to him, So shall your seed be." (Gen. 15:5)

"And he believed in the Lord; and He counted it to him for righteousness." (Gen. 15:6)

"And He said to him, I AM the Lord that brought you out of Ur of the Chaldees to give you this land to inherit it." (Gen. 15:7)

"And he said, Lord God, whereby shall I know that I shall inherit it?" (Gen. 15:8)

"And He said to him, Take me a heifer of three years old, and a she goat of three years old, and a ram of three years old, and a turtledove, and a young pigeon." (Gen. 15:9)

"And he took to him all these, and divided them in the midst and laid each piece one against another: but the birds divided he not" (Gen. 15:10)

"And when the fouls came down upon the carcasses Abram drove them away." (Gen. 15:11)

"And when the sun was going down, a deep sleep fell upon Abram and lo, a horror of great darkness fell upon him." (Gen. 15:12)

"And He said to Abram, know of a surety that your seed shall be a stranger in a land that is not theirs, and shall serve them, and they shall afflict them four hundred years." (Gen. 15:13)

Go Deeper… Get "I Am Sarah's Daughter, How To Get God's Attention In Your Marriage-The Workbook

"And also that nation, whom they shall serve, will I judge; and afterword shall they come out with great substance" (Gen. 15:14)

"And you shall go to your fathers in peace: you shall be buried in a good old age." (Gen. 15:15)

"But in the fourth generation they shall come here again: for the iniquity of the Amorites is not yet full." (Gen. 15:16)

"And it came to pass, that when the sun went down, and it was dark, behold a smoking furnace, and a burning lamp that passed between those pieces." (Gen. 15:17)

"In that same day the Lord made a covenant with Abram saying, Unto your seed have I given this land, from the river of Egypt unto the great river, the river Euphrates;" (Gen. 15:18)

"The Kenites, and the Kenizzites and the Kadmonites" (Gen. 15:19)

"And the Hittites and the Perizzites, and Rephaim" (Gen. 15:20)

"And the Amorites and the Canaanites, and the Girgashites, and the Jebusites. " (Gen. 15:21)

Sarai had to have taken a look at this fourth conversation. Sarai had to have noticed as I did, that not only was it the longest conversation that God had ever had with her husband, but it was also the longest conversation that her husband ever had with God! Sarai must have also noticed that in each of the prior conversations, only God spoke. She had to have noticed that in each of the conversations prior to this conversation, God would speak and Abram would obey. Sarai had to have noticed that outside of God speaking and Abram obeying, there were times that her husband Abram would call upon the name of the Lord but never before was it God speaking then her husband speaking then God speaking! Sarai had to have noticed that for the first time God and Abram were conversing with each other, in a full out conversation, like friends! They were in total communication. Sarai had to have noticed the shift. Sarai had to have taken complete notation of how God initiated the conversation with his salutation or command: "Fear Not, Abram" followed by His promise: "I AM", prefaced by God's name, "your shield, and your exceedingly great reward." (Gen. 15:1)

Sarai had to have noticed that her husband responded with a question: "Lord God, what will you give me, seeing that I go childless, and the steward of my house is this Eliezer of Damascus?" Sarai had to have heard the pain and longing in her husband's conversation with God as Abram continued. "Behold to me you've given no seed: and lo, one born in my house is my heir," (Gen. 15:3) Sarai's heart had to have been breaking as a part of her, as a wife, had to feel that she was the reason that Abram did not have what he wanted. Sarai must have thought," Abram is so distraught that I can't give him a child that that's the first thing he said to God is that I can't have a baby." Of- course we know that that's not what Abram was saying. Abram was in no way complaining about Sarai but imagine how Sarai could have easily interpreted this conversation from Abram. How often as wives do our husbands say something and we take the one thing that he may have said to make a point in one area as injurious to us instead of in the way in which it was intended.

This was the fourth conversation and even though God had given his promise of the seed which gave hope to Sarai before, this time Sarai looked at her husband's words instead of God's. Not only did God reiterate that He would give Abram seed, God went into detail to make it clear that it would not be a servant but it would "come forth out of your own bowels" (Gen. 15:4) God was making it absolutely clear that Abram would have a child that was his own flesh and blood. In verse 5, God went even further to ask Abram to look up into the sky and number the stars, comparing them to the seed that he promised Abram. God commanded Abram to count the stars knowing that for Abram that was impossible showing Abram that He, God could do the impossible. Verse 6 says that Abram responded in action, "He believed in The Lord, and He (The Lord) counted it to him for righteousness." Sarai had to see that Abram's belief in God was an action and God backed it with His own action: He counted it to him for righteousness.

If Sarai was hearing God's words as she did in all of the three previous conversations and taken them as promises to her, Sarai would have listened to the words of her husband as she had in the past, as though God was speaking to her through her husband. Sarai would have heard God speaking directly to her with the promise of the child coming forth from Abram's bowels, as a guaranteed signal to get ready for pregnancy. It was a sign that a baby was coming. Sarai was caught up with the first part of the conversation. Sarai didn't notice that after Abram believed and God counted it to righteousness that God spoke again. Verse 7 continues: God told Abram that He, God brought him from where he was to his present place. Had Sarai heard God's word Sarai would have been reminded of her own testimony and that God had just done the impossible for her. Sarai would have been reminded that God worked miracles for her in Egypt, because she had remained in God's order. Sarai would have been saying, "Oh yeah, that's right, God did deliver me right out of Pharaoh's house. He did send great plagues and got me out because I stayed in His order and trusted Him", but Sarai got lost in the conversation. It seemed as if Sarai stop listening. Sarai had to look as if she was still listening, you know how as wives we nod our heads as our husband is explaining something or as he tells us what happened at work, but we are concentrating on some small detail that he may have mentioned in the beginning of the conversation.

Abram was saying "Honey, then God told me to get a heifer of three years old, and a she goat of three years old and a RAM of three years old, and a turtledove, and a young pigeon." Abram was telling his wife about his day. Abram continued telling how he brought all that God had asked of him and how he laid each piece against the other but he did not divide the bird. Abram told Sarai that after he did the sacrifice, that fowls came down upon the carcasses and Abram drove them away. Abram told Sarai that after he drove them away a deep sleep fell on him. If Sarai was listening she would have noticed that Abram was not told by God to drive the fowls away.

If Sarai was listening, Sarai would have caught the fact that God asked Abram to bring the sacrifice but once the sacrifice was given that it was God's to do as He pleased with the sacrifice. Sarai would have caught the fact that Abram driving the fowls away was Abram doing what he was not told by God to do. And that God was giving her a lesson to see what happens when you don't give him total control and when you take circumstances into your own hands. If she was listening Sarai would have noticed that after her husband did something other than exactly what God told him to do, he was followed by darkness! Abram told Sarai that a deep sleep fell upon Abram and a "horror of great darkness." Sarai would have noticed, if she was listening, that great darkness meant cutting off from great light meaning that Abram had to have displeased God by driving away the fowls because the action was followed by loss of consciousness, followed by great horror which suggests fear followed by darkness, absence of light.

Then judgment is shared by Abram with Sarai. Abram told Sarai that God said, "know of a surety that your seed shall be a stranger in a land that is not theirs and shall serve them: and they shall afflict them for four hundred years." (Gen. 15:13). Sarai, if she was really listening, would have heard that punishment of some sort was falling on Abram's seed. Sarai would have heard that God had just told Abram that his children and grandchildren were going to be slaves! Sarai would have heard that they were going to be afflicted and serving others for four hundred years because of Abram's action. Sarai would have noticed had she been listening, that God does not want just obedience because Abram obeyed by bringing the sacrifice but Abram did not release the sacrifice. How often do we bring something to God but we don't take our hands off of it? Abram brought the sacrifice but he did not take his hands off of it and it displeased God. What are our prayers? Are they not sacrifices? Do you leave what you bring to God with him or do you take it back? Are your hands off of it? If not, it displeases God as it shows a lack of trust in Him which means there is fear which means a lack of faith and "without faith, it's impossible to please God." Heb. 11:6

Abram continued and told Sarai that God also said that He would judge the nation that they would serve and that they would come out with great substance. (Gen. 15:14.) Sarai would have heard God's mercy in what God was saying to Abram "if" Sarai was listening. Sarai would have heard Abram say that God was going to deliver his seed and bless them with great substance. If Sarai had been listening, Sarai would have heard valley and mountain experience on the horizons and Sarai would have received the tools that God was giving, but Sarai was hearing Abram. She was stuck on what Abram said in the beginning of the conversation and Abram did not notice. Sarai was, in a sense, still nodding her head.

Abram continued speaking telling Sarai about his day. Abram continued, then God told me that "You shall go to your fathers in peace: you shall be buried in a good old age". (Gen. 15:15) Abram had just told Sarai that God would be with them throughout their lives! Abram had just shared with Sarai that God had given them assurance of salvation! Sarai missed it! Abram's words poured out of him, telling Sarai about his longest and most informative, detailed and engaging conversation with God. Abram must have said, Sarai, God even told me what would happen after I died. Abram told Sarai that God said, "In the fourth generation they shall come here again: for the iniquity of the Amorites is not yet full." (Gen. 15:16). Sarai was told that when the sun went down and it was dark, Abram saw a smoking furnace and a burning lamp that passed between the pieces" (Gen. 15:17) Abram was telling Sarai about a miracle in the midst of a miracle! Abram closed off his conversation with Sarai sharing the best part. Abram shared that God made a covenant promising them seed and land." (Gen. 15:18)

Abram had to be thrilled. If Sarai had been listening Sarai would have received the confirmations and lessons, promises and tools along with assurance from God's words through her husband, but Sarai got stuck. Sarai heard her husband words instead of God's. Sarai, instead of fixating her heart on, 'Fear not, I am your shield' and 'you will have a child and it will come from your bowels' and reassurance that Abram would be saved, Sarai got stuck on her husband's words and made it about her. Honestly, we can all relate. Imagine that your husband says to you, "Babe I just had the longest conversation with God! Babe, He told me to Fear not and he'd be my shield and I asked, "what can you give me God, seeing that I don't even have a child."

If you weren't able to have a child yet, how many of us would not take it personally? How many of us would hear it in "Girl" translation, "God seriously, my wife can't even give me a baby so why are we even having this conversation?" Or "Supergirl" translation, "If you had given me a wife that could get pregnant I'd be good," or "supersized real girl" translation "It's my wife's fault!" Whether you hear it in "Girl", "Supergirl" or "Supersized Real Girl", you'd probably take it personally and that could obstruct the ability to see clearly. How often have you heard that things can be lost in the translation? The true essence of Abram's statement can be lost in a translation. Is it possible that the same is possible when we translate our husband's conversation into "girl?" Is it possible that blame can be added to the translation when it absolutely was not there in the first place? Is it possible that Abram was in problem solution conversation and he wasn't bashing his wife? Is it possible that Abram was speaking out of a heart for his wife? Is it possible that Abram may have been thinking, 'here I am having a conversation with God, the fixer of everything, let me tell him what I need fixed?' Is it possible that Abram presented what meant the most to the person that meant the most to him? What if Sarai made the assumption that her husband was just problem-solving with the ultimate problem solver? What if Sarai trusted that God had her heart and she trusted that her husband's heart was in the right place and that even if it wasn't she would remain committed to God's order and trust God.

Not this time. Sarai clearly made a shift in conversation four that Abram had with God. Instead of grasping hold on to the words of the Lord, Sarai grabbed a hold onto her husband's words and look at what happened next... When we let go of God's words and step out of order we begin to seek our own solutions because we entertain doubt and fear. When we entertain doubt we aren't trusting God to give us what we desire and we fear that we won't get the desires of our heart which is the exact opposite of God's word. His word says that "He will give us the desire of our hearts." Psalms 37:4

Sarai had taken her mind off of God's word allowing fear and doubt, the exact opposite of God's word in the conversation that He had just had with her husband. Chapter 16 begins with the focus shift from God's promises to what Sarai could see. A shift was made in her circumstances. It suggests a different Sarai, "the Sarai Now", or "Now Sarai". It's interesting that the next sentence begins with the word "now" as opposed to "then" or how it was before. This is the first signal that a shift had taken place in Sarai. "Now Sarai, Abram's wife bore him no children". (Gen. 16:1) Please note that this fact had existed previously but Sarai was committed to remaining in order but once she took her focus off of God's words and placed her focus on her husband's words, Sarai stepped out of order. Sarai was focusing on her husband's words. Sarai decided to step out of order above Abram and took the answer to her "problem" into her own hands. Even the wording shows this to us, it starts out with "now Sarai", followed by the problem, "bore him no children: and" that "and" brought someone else into the equation. That "and" showed that not only had Sarai stepped out of order but she was willing to solve her "problem" herself. Again, let me say that Sarai should have remained in order under the exact same circumstances however, due to her shift in focus from God's word to her husband's words, Sarai made the decision to take things into her own hands.

Genesis 16:1 shows the shift. "Now" (states the time), "Sarai" (states the person), "Abram's wife" (states the position), "bore him no children" (states the problem): (before these two dots is stated the exact situation that existed in Genesis 11:30 with the exception of the position. In Gen. 11:30, it states that Sarai was barren, but between Gen. 11:30 and Gen. 16:1 Sarai's position had been established supernaturally by God in her deliverance out of Pharaoh's house. Unfortunately, Sarai had forgotten. Sarai had allowed that powerful supernatural delivery to become faint and dim in her memory. Maybe Sarai had no one that she chose to tell her testimony. Maybe that was the reason she forgot what the Egyptians knew, that The God of Abram and Sarai could do anything! Those two dots showed that Sarai allowed her testimony to lapse in her own mind. How often do we do the same thing? God does something absolutely amazing and it's something that is so miraculous that there is no question that it was the Very Hand of God. We may shout Hallelujah and tell a friend or two then another problem shows up in our lives and we totally forget the miracle. We may allow the power of the miracle to lapse in our memory instead of encouraging us that we have the miracle as evidence that The God that delivered us out of our "Pharaoh's House," can deliver us out of the next circumstance no matter what it may be.

Sarai was seeing one thing, "her circumstance" and she decided to step out of order. Sarai decided to add her own solution. Those two dots (colons) brought something that was not intended by God, the "And". "And she had a handmaid, an Egyptian, whose name was Hagar". There was no "And" in God's plan for Abram and Sarai. Let's take a closer look at chapter 16:1, it's the verse where everything turns around. Notice that Genesis 16:1 has no one in that verse except Sarai. The verse depicts the perfect "all about me" mentality. The verse speaks of Sarai. The verse speaks about what Sarai did not have and then it suggests what she had. The verse gives the total line of thinking of Sarai. I can almost hear Sarai thinking out loud, "Well let's see, I don't have children but I do have a handmaid I could. ..." Before you can even hear her next thought, we find ourselves in verse 2 and Sarai saying something to Abram. "Behold, a.k.a. "now look", "The Lord has restrained me from bearing" translation, "Babe, look obviously God didn't mean what he said about us having a baby at least not through me so Babe please go into Hagar, get her pregnant so that I can have a child!" It sounds crazy even as I write it. You would think that Abram would have said "Babe, are you serious? Girl, do you hear yourself? You're saying that you don't believe God. You're asking me to bring someone else into our marriage! Babe, I'm sorry but I can't."

But no. That one "And" led to another "And." First there was "And …….. Hagar" then there was "And Abram." "And Abram hearkened to the voice of Sarai." Sarai's thoughts moved into words then into action all outside of the will of God. Sarai created her own solution to get what God had promised, only further creating another problem. Just a sidebar, I often wondered why there was no objection spoken from Abram, maybe Abram was shocked that Sarai would suggest such a thing or maybe it was the fact that Abram was tired of waiting as well, or maybe it was because Hagar was a beautiful African woman, wait a minute Egypt is in Africa, right?;) I'm double checking the geography. Yes, Egypt is in Africa and maybe it was a combination of all three but either way the plan was put into place because Sarai lost sight of everything except her circumstance and decided not to wait on God. Sarai implemented her own solution.

Maybe the real reason that Abram hearkened unto Sarai is because this is the very first place noted that Sarai spoke! As a matter of fact, one can say this is the only time Sarai really spoke up until this time. If a person is of a few words, when they do speak most people listen to them because when they do speak it's assumed to be of value and importance. Maybe Abram hearkened because Abram knew his wife Sarai to be of the character not to ever step out of order so when she did, it held weight. Whatever the reason we know from verse 3 that

Sarai stepped out of order and gave Hagar, her handmaid, to Abram to be his wife. Note in verse 4 that Sarai took full control.

1. Sarai looked at her circumstance.

2. Sarai looked at her handmaid Hagar as a solution.

3. Sarai convinced Abram to sleep with Hagar

4. Sarai, "took Hagar her maid, the Egyptian... And gave her to her husband to be his wife." Gen. 16:3

Imagine the level of desperation that Sarai had to have been feeling in an order for her to give her own husband another woman to be his wife! That's what happens when we take our eyes off of God and His promises and we focus on our circumstances. Desperation steps in, then it swells and engulfs all hope of God's deliverance. In order for Sarai to get in such a place of desperation Sarai had to have taken her eyes off of God's words. Sarai had to take her eyes off of God's promises. Sarai had to step out of order in order to take things into her own hands. Note that Sarai did not just step out of the order that God created and established:

God

Husband

Wife

Sarai stepped into a different order. We would each assume that Sarai moved out of order creating the following order:

God

Wife

Husband

but that is not the order that Sarai created. Sarai created a new order. Sarai stepped out of order and created the order below:

Wife

Husband

God

Or so she thought, but The New Order is the order that Sarai created:

Wife

Husband

Sarai's New Order took God out of the solution completely and Sarai replaced God, the provider of promises with herself! Sarai had taken God's place! Sarai caused her husband to question God's word. Sarai convinced her husband to allow her to be his provider of promise. Sarai convinced Abram to accept her solution. Sarai stepped into the place of God! Sarai caused both herself and her husband to be "out of order." Sarai's solution could not be implemented unless it was "out of order".

Why is it that even as I write I'm struck with such a bone chilling presence of similarity? Where have I heard this before? Where have I seen where a woman, a wife, questions God's promises and causes her husband to do the same? "Babe did God say that?"... And the verse even begins the same. "Now the serpent was more subtle than any beast of the field, which the Lord God had made. And he said to the woman, "Yea, has God said, You shall not eat of every tree of the garden?" (Gen. 3:1). Notice how sin began with questioning God's word? Not only did sin begin with the questioning of God's word, it began with bringing in a fourth party into the relationship. There was God, Adam and Eve but out of nowhere there is a fourth; an "AND" added: the serpent. We see Eve stepping out of the order set up by God and moving into the role of leading her husband astray. Eve provides for Adam after convincing him to question, disobey and step "out of order" of God's word. Eve took God out of the equation and took the lead.

The questioning God's word or his promises is the first step in stepping out of order and creating sin. Stepping out in front of the husband, Sarai followed the same template or pattern. Sarai brought in a fourth party, Hagar into the relationship that God intended to be just, God, Abram and Sarai, in that order. Once a fourth person was involved, the husband is convinced by the wife, through the questioning of God's word, that maybe God didn't mean what He said. In the place of God's word is the solution as presented by the wife via the fourth party. In order to orchestrate the solution as posed by Sarai, God's word had to be questioned. Doubt had to be raised in the suggestion of "maybe God meant," had to be imposed. God, His promises, His solution and faith must be removed and replaced with the wife as the head and her solution as to what God had in mind. The husband has to be convinced that God did not mean what He said and He could not be trusted. The word of the wife had to become more trustworthy and dependable than God's word. God and

His word had to be doubted and removed. Sarai had taken her focus off of God's word and she had to convince her husband to do the same in order for her solution to take God's place. Sarai had done just that. Sarai used the gift of influence that she had on her husband to convince him that he could not trust God to give her a child and that another party needed to be brought into the marriage.

Even as I write The Holy Ghost keeps impressing upon me how careful we as wives/women must be with our words and influence. Sarai had not just convinced Abram but she also convinced Hagar. Sarai was totally out of order but she had implemented her solution. "And he went into Hagar, and she conceived: and when she saw that she had conceived, her mistress was despised in her eyes." (Gen. 16:4). Which one of you are surprised? Imagine you bring a young beautiful Egyptian woman into your home to surrogate a child for your husband and yourself. They conceive and she doesn't care for you once she discovers that she's pregnant. Would you be surprised? It would make sense that she realizes that her time clock is ticking down to the time of nine months. She has to realize that one of the women after the baby is born will become obsolete and it wouldn't take much to figure out who that would be. Imagine the servants that Hagar once lodged with in their tents are now saying, "Hagar is carrying Abram's child." Hagar is eating better than she's ever eaten.

Her clothing is of a finer quality. She has the company of this powerful man Abram and she is aware that it was not intended forever. Hagar's status has changed and so has her countenance towards her mistress because Hagar must be thinking, "Hmmm, she's Abram's wife, I'm Abram's wife. We are on the same level. Hence, the despising. Hagar thought herself more than she was. In Sarai's eyes, Hagar was a means to an end. Hagar was a solution. Hagar was also a reminder that Sarai had taken things into her own hands. Hagar was a reminder that Sarai had stepped out of order. Hagar was now a solution that needed to be controlled.

How often do we find ourselves in Sarai's position? Anytime we replace God's solution with our own and question His word we find ourselves where Sarai found herself. Anytime we change God's order and/or step out of order it never fares as planned and we have to repent and run back to God and our husbands and eat humble pie. I just think humble pie should have at least another flavor, like chocolate, but it doesn't and it's hard to swallow. We've all had a slice or two. Sarai was right there with a napkin on her lap around her neck and a fork in her hand as you can see in verse 5 of chapter 16. "And Sarai said to Abram, My wrong be upon you: I have given my maid into your bosom: and when she saw that she had conceived, I was despised in her eyes: the Lord judge between me and you." (Gen. 16:5). Here now is Sarai owning her wrong. Sarai says she made a mistake and confesses her wrong and the consequence. She is attempting to get Abram to lead in this situation now that it's out of order and now she mentions the Lord. But Abram is not trying to lead or get involved in the matter. Look at verse 6 "But, Abram said to Sarai, Behold, your maid is in your hand; do to her as it pleases you. And when Sarai dealt hardly (or harshly) with her, she fled from her face." (Gen. 16:6). For whatever reason Abram did not want to get involved between these two women. Abram put the responsibility back on Sarai. Abram was not taking anything else into his hands!

Have you ever gotten out of order by moving forward with your own solution and then had to go back to your husband to ask him to fix it for you and he says, "No babe, I think you should see it through to the end." It's not a good feeling. Before God taught me the principle of being Sarai's daughter, I wore this dress in several colors. I would say, "Babe" and he'd say "Babe if you had asked me 'before' you…" Finish the blank, and I'd have to figure it out. "I must say that though I wore that dress if he had taken whatever I had taken on without him, I would not have stopped and on my own burned the "dresses_Abram did not switch places with Sarai. It was almost as if his action was saying, "No Babe, you wanted to be out in front so I'm letting you be out in front. You wanted to lead." Abram allowed Sarai to stay in her chosen position. Abram allowed Sarai to deal with Hagar and the consequences. "Sarai dealt harshly with her and she fled from her face." (Gen. 16:6). Let's slow this story down and read between the lines just a little. Imagine Sarai is with Hagar and Sarai knows Hagar is carrying her husband's child, his heir. Sarai has to be excited as she sees Hagar's stomach growing. Sarai has to want to connect with the baby by wanting to touch Hagar's stomach. Imagine Sarai wanting to feel the baby kick. Imagine Hagar running, okay not running, wobbling quickly to Abram and saying the baby just moved and Abram places his hand on Hagar's stomach. Imagine Sarai seeing the scene rushes up to feel the baby move and Hagar moves away. Imagine Sarai seeing Abram laughing with Hagar over the movement of the baby and sharing her excitement about the child's birth and Sarai not being allowed to be involved. Imagine the mixed feelings that Sarai experienced after being the only woman in her husband's life for so many years then to see another woman with her husband and being "despised" by the woman. Imagine how Sarai felt after she treated Hagar harshly and Hagar runs away with the baby in her womb. Imagine the anguish, regret, disappointment, embarrassment and shame, coupled with worry and loss that Sarai must have felt when she realized that Hagar fled because of her and she did not know her whereabouts.

Go Deep Get "I Am Sarah's Daughter, How To Get God's Attention In Your Marriage-The Workbook

Anytime we step out of God's order it is followed by heartache that God never intended for us. But God is full of compassion. Look at verse 7 "And the angel of the Lord found her by a fountain of water in the wilderness, by the fountain in the way to Shur." Note that we are given no indication as to how long Hagar was gone. Verse 8 "And He said, Hagar, Sarai's maid, where came you? And where will you go?" Notice how Hagar is called by her name but she is also addressed by her title! This indicated without a doubt that the angel was making it clear that though Hagar was carrying Abram's child her position, her title, and her status in Heaven's eyes had not changed. To all of Heaven, Hagar was still Hagar and she was still Sarai's maid. The angel could have easily just called her Hagar and continued with what He was saying but the angel was not just sent to find Hagar on behalf of Sarai; the angel was sent to put Hagar back in her place both geographically as well as psychologically. Hagar was reminded through this conversation with the angel that she was

Sarai's maid. "Sarai, Abram's wife took Hagar her maid the Egyptian, and gave her to her husband Abram to be his wife" --- Heaven saw Hagar as Sarai's maid! Let's dissect that a little further. When I was in elementary school we had to underline the noun in a sentence and a verb as well as the adjective and adverb. We would underline showing possession or "belonging to." In Genesis 16:3 if I were doing that elementary homework, it would look like this:

And   Sarai, Abram's wife

↑   noun   adjective

in addition

conjunction

took   Hagar   her   maid

verb   noun   adjective

action   possessive   describing

word

the Egyptian...   and   gave

adjective	conjunction	verb
describing Hagar		action

her	to	her
pronoun	preposition	
pronoun		
taking the		taking
the		
place of	(links a noun	place
of		
the noun,	to another	Sarai
Hagar	word)	

husband	actually	her husband

ABRAM WOULD NOT BE DIVIDED

114

the

her is still referring to Sarai

Abbreviated

meaning…   Sarai,
Abram's wife

                                                                    noun 1.

Possessive

established

took   Hagar…   Her maid
and

verb   noun   3. Possessive
established

2. Action

gave   her   to   her husband

verb   pronoun possessive established

Abram   "to be"   his wife.

Not established

Sarai, is the initiator.

Abram's wife, is her title and her position.

It is established.

Sarai, took - action taken by Sarai.

Hagar, her maid - Hagar, name

Her, possessive, belonging to Sarai

maid - title

gave - action

her- Hagar- the maid

to -

her husband - Her - Sarai's husband -

Sarai's husband

the positions that were established were as follows:

Sarai - Abram's wife

Abram - Her, (Sarai's) husband

Hagar Her (Sarai's) maid.

That which was established by God was as follows:

Sarai   -   established as "the wife."

When Sarai was taken by the Pharaoh in Egypt and plagued by the Lord, Sarai was established as "the wife" of Abram. Gen. 18: "The Pharaoh said… "Why did you not tell me that she was your wife?"

Your - Possessive belonging to: Abram "so I might have taken her to me as a wife"

Notice that "a" wife is not possessive.

"Behold, your wife" - possessive

"take her"- possessive pronoun

20 "and sent him away and his wife"

Possessive   - belonging to.

Sarai's possession as "wife" - "the wife" was established by God.

"And Abram went out of Egypt, he and his wife - note: he and "his wife" - possessive and established.

Sarai's position as "wife" was not established by Abram. Sarai's position as wife was not established by Sarai. Sarai's position as wife was established by God.

Therefore even Sarai could not transfer or change the position. Hagar was Sarai's maid. Hagar belonged to Sarai. Hagar's position was maid. Sarai attempted to change Hagar's position by giving Hagar, her maid, to Abram, Sarai's husband, "to be" his wife, but the position of wife was already established and filled. More importantly the position and title was not given to Sarai by Sarai. Sarai did not have the authority to give the position of wife to Hagar, the maid, neither could she establish the title hence the language of the angel. Sarai was out of order and then got Hagar out of order and the angel came on Sarai's behalf to put things back in order. The Angel's language is clear. He does not call Hagar, Abram's wife! He calls Hagar by her name and by her position and title. He told her who she was by reminding her. "Hagar, Sarai's maid."

Translation in girl, "don't get it twisted. You may be pregnant with Abram's baby but sweetie, you're a pregnant maid! Your position has not changed, just your attitude, which I'm here to adjust and your figure will go back to where it was before, shortly." Just in case there was still some confusion in Hagar's thinking, the angel made things really clear. "Return to your

119

mistress, and submit yourself under her hands." (Gen. 16:9) Notice the angel told Hagar to return to her "mistress" the person that had authority over her. The angel did not once refer to Abram, instead the angel addressed Hagar strictly on behalf of Sarai and her position in relationship to Sarai. The angel gives no acknowledgment to Hagar being in any way a possession of Abram's. The angel makes no recognition of establishment of Hagar as a wife instead the angel reiterates her position as a maid and her ownership by Sarai. To make sure that there was absolutely no confusion Abram's name did not come out of the angel's mouth! No marriage was mentioned or acknowledged. It was almost as if Sarai had not taken any action! The angel continued His conversation with Hagar after establishing her name and title and position, he makes it clear who has authority over Hagar. Conversation between the angel and Hagar was as if the angel was speaking strictly on behalf of Sarai!

The angel continues and the subject matter changes after Hagar has been commanded to return to Sarai. The angel addresses the child that Hagar is carrying. "I will multiply your seed exceedingly, that it shall not be numbered for multitude."(Gen.

16:10) The angel then gets more personal. The conversation seemed to soften. "Behold, you are with child and shall bear a son, and shall call his name Ishmael: because The Lord has heard your affliction." (Gen. 16:11) This is the only time that there is recognition that there has been affliction but it is not removed, just recognized. The final aspect of the conversation addressed the future of the child. "He will be a wild man, his hand will be against every man, and every man's hand against him, and he shall dwell in the presence of his brethren." (Gen. 16:12) The angel also shares the sex of the child, his name and its meaning.

Sarai had taken things into her own hands and brought in Hagar, a "fourth" party into her marriage. Things did not turn out as Sarai planned or hoped. How often do we step out of God's order and like Sarai and take things into our own hands only to be disappointed by the outcome? Sarai had stepped out of order and created a heart wrenching situation or what some would refer to as "drama". Hagar returned to Sarai and gave birth to a son, Ishmael. Abram was eighty-six years old. Thirteen years passed until the next recorded conversation between God and Abram. Thirteen years then the sixth conversation. It was really the fifth conversation. The celestial conversation prior to this conversation had taken place because of Sarai but not with Sarai or Abram. Sarai had watched and heard the second-hand account of conversations that Abram had with God, yet she was never involved. Sarai had to have noticed that God had become silent for some time with her husband. Even though Sarai was not having the types of conversations with God as her husband Abram, the idea of knowing that God is speaking to your husband had to bring Sarai some delight. It must have been inspirational. Sarai had to, like Abram, been aware of the silence.

God's Fifth Conversation with Abram

Finally, the silence is broken and God speaks. It's been thirteen years and God speaks to Abram. Genesis chapter 17 begins with the conversation. "And when Abram was ninety years old and nine, the Lord appeared to Abram, and said to him. "I AM the Almighty God: walk before Me, and be you perfect. And I will make my covenant between Me and you, and it will multiply you exceedingly." (Gen. 17: 1-2) "And Abram fell on his face: and God talked with him saying, 'As for Me, behold. My covenant is with you, and you shall be a father of many nations. Neither shall your name anymore be called Abram, but your name shall be Abraham, for a father of many nations have I made you. And I

122

will make you exceedingly fruitful and I will make nations of you and Kings shall come out of you. And I will establish My covenant between Me and you and your seed after you in their generations for an everlasting covenant, to be a God to you and your seed after you. And I will give to you and your seed after you, the land where in you are a stranger, all the Land of Canaan for an everlasting possession; and I will be their God.' (Gen. 17:3-8) "And God said to Abraham, 'You shall keep My covenant therefore, you and your seed after you in their generations. This is My covenant, which you shall keep between Me and you and your seed after you; Every man child among you shall be circumcised, and you shall circumcise the flesh of your foreskin; and it shall be a token of the covenant between Me and you. And he that is eight days old shall be circumcised among you, every man child in your generations, he that is born in the house or bought with money of any stranger, which is not of your seed. He that is born in your house and he that is bought with your money must needs be circumcised and My covenant shall be in your flesh for an everlasting covenant. And the uncircumcised man child whose flesh of his foreskin is not circumcised, that soul shall be cut off from his people; he has broken My covenant.'" (Gen. 17:9-14)

"And God said to Abraham. 'As for Sarai your wife, you shall not call her name Sarai but Sarah shall her name be. "And I will bless her and give you a son also of her, yea I will bless her and she shall be a mother of nations; Kings of people shall be of her.'" (Gen. 9:15-16) "Then Abraham fell upon his face and laughed and said in his heart, shall a child be born to him that is 100 years old? And shall Sarah, that is 90 years old, bear? And Abraham said to God, O that Ishmael might live before you! And God said, "Sarah your wife shall bear you a son indeed; and you shall call his name Isaac; and I will establish My covenant with him for an everlasting covenant and with his seed after him. And as for Ishmael I have heard you: Behold I have blessed him, and will make him fruitful and will multiply him exceedingly; twelve princes shall he father; and I will make him a great nation. (Gen. 17: 17-20) But My covenant will I establish with Isaac, which Sarah shall bear to you at this set time in the next year."

124

And He left off talking with him and God went up from Abraham. (Gen. 21-22)

What a conversation! God came to speak to Abraham after thirteen years of silence and had a lot to say: First: The conversation is initiated by God. Second: He is clear and direct. He gives to Abraham instruction and promises but there is a gentleness that I hear in his tone towards Abraham and especially Sarah. God shows up announcing who He is and His authority.

What a way to break the silence!

"I AM The Almighty God"

He states His title covered in majesty and unmistakable power!!!

Then He gives His command:

"Walk before Me and Be you perfect"

Look at the beauty of Abraham's response: Abraham fell on his face. Imagine Abram's awe… His feeling of relief to know that God was visiting him again.

Imagine God being silent in your life after you've made a mistake… for a long time. Imagine not hearing from Him or maybe not feeling his presence. I would have fallen on my face as well…I would have had tears of joy and relief coupled with fear of reverence at the fact that The Most High God was visiting me after I had made a mistake. Not only does God come back to Abraham but God is not showing up empty-handed. God shows up and is offering to make a pact, a deal, a contract times a million, God his offering a covenant! He's offering something that is stronger than a pact, stronger than a deal, and stronger than a contract. God is offering a covenant that is sealed in blood! Yes, it is blood from a foreskin but it is blood nonetheless.

God is offering to join Himself to Abram after Abram and Sarai went contrary to God's plan. What mercy! What love! Think about it, you are clear in your direction with someone and they go the opposite way from your direction. Would you show up next time you see them with a lifelong contract to secure their services? Probably not. If anything, you'd probably be explaining to them that you no longer need their services! You would most likely not hand them a bonus at that time but that's exactly what God did for Abram! God shows up and offers Abram a life time partnership with him. Not only does God show up with an offer to a lifetime unbreakable covenant but God is also bearing gifts and promises. God is offering to multiply Abram "exceedingly." That means that God will not do it in a small way! God also tells Abram that not only is He going to make Abram a father of many nations, He, God is changing Abram's name to Abraham which means "Father of many nations". God then tells Abraham again in another way. God tells Abraham that God will make him "exceedingly fruitful," He continues by telling Abraham that not only will he be multiplied but that Kings will come out of him.

I can just feel God's excitement and love as He shares this news of promise and gifts with Abraham. I love giving gifts! I get excited and almost giddy as I wrap them and display them to give the person that I'm planning to surprise. While I love receiving gifts I can say that it's truly more fun getting a gift together to give to someone else. I plan the colors based on their preference. I consider their personality. I consider what they like and don't like and I enjoy every moment of shopping and planning that leads to that single moment of when that person takes the package out of my hands into their hands and they begin to unwrap the gift with anticipation. I'm sharing equal excitement as they pull out the tissue paper and lift the item out of the bag. I'm all lit up as they unwrap the present. With each removal of the tape from the wrapping paper, I'm bursting inside! I'm more excited to see their response to the gift than they are to see the gift! No moment of planning leading up to the unveiling of the gift is wasted!

I believe this is what God was feeling! As a matter of fact, I believe that from the time Abraham and Sarah made the mistake God was working on this reveal! I believe the moment that they went another way God couldn't wait to show them what He really had for them and how much better it would be than their way. I believe that God broke the silence with love! Let me show you how I know this to be so. The same way that God sent an angel to put Hagar back on track could have been used with Abram. God could have sent a messenger, celestial of course, but messenger just the same, but instead, the Almighty God himself camel. What an honor that was and what an amazing display of love. Why did He come instead of sending an angel? Imagine that you picked out the most beautiful gift for someone. You have wrapped it in the most exquisite wrapping fit for a queen. The bow is delicate and soft. It is made of the finest silk. Not only is the wrapping gorgeous but the gift bag is elegant and echoes luxury. After all of the preparation is complete you call a messenger to deliver the gift to the person. In addition, you and the person for whom you have purchased and prepared the gift, have not spoken in thirteen years. Now imagine if you were the person for whom the gift was meant. No matter how beautiful and extravagant the gift, would it have meant more if it was presented to you by the person with whom you had not spoken? Wouldn't it remove that feeling of I wonder if everything is really good between us? That's exactly what God's actions eliminated. God, The Almighty delivering the gift, a covenant, and the promises directly to Abraham complete with a name change. Do you see the love?

In verse 7 of chapter 17 God continues by saying "I will be a God to you and your seed"! That is such a declaration of love from God to Abraham. It shows that God is really pouring Himself out in love for this man Abraham and his wife! The promise that He will be his God is magnanimous. That promise is more than anything. God is promising Himself to Abraham! It's taking some wrapping of my mind around that! My heart is passed full at the thought. God follows up in verse 8 by the gift and promise of land and reaffirming that He, God, will be Abraham's God.

After God gives promises and confirmation He explains the detail of the circumcision covenant, including Abraham, complete with the age: every child eight days old. I found that interesting because the number eight represents new beginnings!!! I wondered why men had to be circumcised, when Sarah made the mistake. I wondered if the circumcision covenant would have been put in place had the mistake not been made. I also wondered if the sacrifice being made by the men was because they were the head. All these questions are food for thought. It may seem that the woman made no sacrifice but I'm sure that it was not easy for the Israelite women to hand over their eight-day-old baby boys for circumcision. God was clear that whether bought or born from seed, it was required, and there would be no exceptions. God went as far as saying that any man child sold who did not undergo circumcision, would have his soul cut off.

Theologians often compare the circumcision to the circumcision of the heart. The circumcision of the heart, meaning allowing the heart to be wholly surrendered to God. The circumcision of the heart is not limited to the male but is warranted of both male and female. The heart then that would not be fully surrendered to God would then be cut off. The soul would be cut off from God. It makes sense. A soul whose heart is on not surrendered would be lost, cut off eternally.

This is for me the absolute best part of the conversation. In verses 15-16, God has a special word… "As for Sarai, your wife, you shall not call her name Sarai; but Sarah shall her name be. And I will bless her and give you a son also of her; yea, I will bless her and she shall be a mother of nations: Kings of people

131

shall be of her." I'm so full of joy and awe at God right now and you will be too when I show you what just happened! Following the explanation of the rules associated with circumcision, God turned the conversation from Abraham to Sarah. God already established: "I will bless "you" and I will make a covenant with "you" I will bring Kings out of "you" I will give the land to "you", now He declared: "As for Sarai, your wife"... The – the definitions of "as for" are as follows:

1. With respect to
2. On the subject of
3. In the matter of
4. As regards to
5. Regarding
6. With reference to

The Almighty God was in a Boardroom meeting with Abraham. He had gone over every topic that He chose to address and He had now arrived at the final subject of discussion. It was to be addressed clearly and with authority. It was the final topic but not the least important.

The Almighty God had made a move from discussing Abraham to discussing Sarai. The All-Knowing, All-Powerful, All-seeing God had taken special note of Sarai. The "All" Powerful God began his conversation concerning Sarai…

As for Sarai:

concerning Sarai

with respect to Sarai

on the subject of Sarai

in the matter of Sarai

as regards to Sarai

regarding Sarai

with reference to Sarai

God calls Sarai by her name! It is the first time that the Almighty God had called Sarai by name!!! Not only did God call Sarai by name but the Almighty God is speaking about

Sarai with authority. The Almighty God is speaking up for Sarai, the Almighty God is not just speaking about Sarai, the Almighty God is speaking on Sarai's behalf and there is authority and no-nonsense in His tone. The Almighty speaks about her and for her to her husband, Abraham. The Almighty calls Sarai by her name and then by her title to Abraham. Then The Most High God gives Abraham a command regarding Sarai. The Most High God commands Abraham NOT to call her Sarai but Sarah. God says in a command to Abraham in translation... Concerning Sarai you are not allowed to call her Sarai, Sarah is her name, in other words I've changed her name as well. Then God adds in an "AND" with a promise that was finally personal for Sarai. A promise that was so clear that there was no room for confusion or any man made or woman made solutions. God continues in verse 16 of Genesis with:

#1 "I will bless her"

2 "And give you a son also of her"

3 "yea or yes"

[Before you say no-I'm saying yes. God repeats Himself.]

#4 "I will bless her."

#5 "and she shall be a mother of nations."

#6 "Kings of people shall be of her."

God has given His full attention toward Sarai and He has been clear in giving a command that Abraham is <u>NOT</u> allowed to call her Sarai. God announces that He, God, The Almighty has changed Sarai's name as well is Abraham's. God also announces that He is going to bless her and that Sarah is going to bare a son, and that Sarah is going to be a mother of nations and that Kings would come forth from her.

Let's examine the response.

Abraham fell on his face and laughed.

Abraham had not heard from The Most High God in 13 years. The Almighty God breaks His 13-year silence and comes to speak to Abraham. The Almighty God promises Abraham's seed and land. He offers him a covenant and He offers him exclusivity in being His God. Abraham listens to the long lists of blessings coming his way, according to The Word of God with respect and reverence. As a matter of fact, Abraham is respectfully on his face before God, but the moment that God spoke blessings over Sarah, Abraham was unable to receive, believe or acknowledge the blessing. When God was speaking to Abraham about, blessing Abraham with seed, the number of the grains of sand, Abraham could believe it. When God said his seed would be more than the stars, Abraham could accept it but the moment the blessing involved God blessing His wife, Abraham had no faith or respect for that possibility. The moment the Blessing included Sarah, it became a joke! It causes a question to rise-

Did Abraham believe the multitude would come out of Ishmael?

Did Abraham believe that he would have another Hagar?

Or did Abraham believe that the seed that God was promising would be coming out of someone else? Is it possible that Abraham just felt that Sarah had no reason to hope or dream anymore? Is it possible that the closest person to Sarah that knew her dream, thought that the time for her dream had come and gone?

Some of you may have a dream, a hope, a desire that God will bless you with something. You may have been waiting for a long time. You may be waiting longer than some and others who may be close to you may have given up on your dreams. They may have stopped believing for you and they may even have stopped believing in you. In their hearts they may be laughing but I want to tell you that when you become Sarah's daughter you don't have to worry about anyone believing in your dreams because God will step in. You don't have to worry about how much time has passed since the conception of the dream, God will birth it.

Abraham could receive blessings for himself but he could not believe for Sarah. Others may feel that God will come through for them but not for you. You may even be like Sarah, it may be your husband that doesn't or can't believe for you. He may laugh in his heart or even in your face but I'm here to tell you that The Almighty is not laughing. The Almighty, as long as you remain Sarah's daughter will speak up for you. Even if you are like Sarah and the rest of us, and you have failed him and at times made a mess trying to make a solution, God still believes in you and will do the impossible for you.

Genesis 17:17 says, "Then Abraham fell on his face, and laughed, and said in his heart, "Shall a child be born to him that is a hundred years old?" And shall Sarah, that is ninety years old, bare?" Abraham, when Sarah is thrown in the equation, asks if a man who is a hundred years old should have a child but that question was not raised to God by Abraham from verses 1-14 of Chapter 17, when all of those promises included seed. Then Abraham asks about Sarah. Can she have a child at ninety? Abraham, after disbelieving, gives God his solution. Notice that Abraham is giving Ishmael as a solution in the same way that Sarai offered Hagar as a solution. Is Abraham following Sarah?

"And Abraham said to God" O that Ishmael might live before you." (Gen. 17:18) Abraham is presenting Ishmael as his solution. God redirects and refocuses Abraham. Genesis 17:19 states, "and God said, "Sarah, your wife shall bear you a son indeed, and you shall call his name Isaac: and I will establish my covenant with him for an everlasting covenant, and with his seed after him."

God is clear. God is definitive. He calls Sarah's name again and is crystal clear that Sarah will have a son and who will be the covenant son. In other words, "I'm telling you what I'm doing through Sarah. I am honoring her." God continues in verse 20 and addresses Abraham's solution of Ishmael. God says, "I have heard you." Stop right there. Did you get that? God told Abraham, "I heard you! I have blessed him and will make him fruitful, and will multiply him exceedingly; twelve Princes shall he beget, and I will make him a great nation."

God completes His sentence then says "<u>But</u>" When God says, "But!" He's not playing. God was saying let me make Myself clear, "Abraham I heard you. I blessed Ishmael. But My covenant will come through Sarah."

Let's read it "But My covenant will I establish with Isaac which Sarah shall bear to you at this set time in the next year." God, The Almighty, stood up for Sarah. The Almighty called her by name five times! The Almighty said "her "in reference to her six times and The Almighty God said, "she", once. Sarah was spoken of by The Almighty 12 times!!! The Almighty God said that it would happen in 12 months!!

12 times

12 months

Then The Almighty God put a period. Look at verse 22: "And He left off talking with him and God went up from

Abraham." In other words, God told Abraham I'm going to bless Sarah with a son, My covenant. I don't care how old she is. He referenced her 12 times then said it will happen in 12 months... Followed by verse 22 translated into... And that's final! "Left off talking with him!"

God had spoken and then said that's it! He walked out of the Boardroom. What a powerful scene God had just displayed. God left no questions about His feelings for Sarah. God broke His silence with great news and personal news. God shows Himself in such a personal way. God, The Almighty, was conversing and even reasoning with Abraham but He was not negotiable when it came to Sarah. God had made His mind up about honoring Sarah. God had decided to use Sarah to bless Abraham. God had decided to give Sarah the desires of her heart and God did not care about the time or her age. God began with a command to Sarah's husband telling him you are not allowed to call her Sarai – "You shall not", it was a command. It was spoken with the same verbiage as the commandments. – "Thou shall not... kill, or steal" etc. It was a strong command from God telling Abraham do not address her as Sarai or her former self. I, The Almighty have promoted her. I AM, changed her name. Every time you call her name she will be reminded that I fight for her. Every time she hears her new name, she will know that she is special to me. Every time you call her name, she will be reminded that the promise of a child, a son, is coming and she is my vessel whom I have chosen. Every time she hears her name, she will be reminded that I don't need her help to bring about my word. Every time you call her name she will remember that I love her. Every time she hears her name, she will know that she and she alone is the woman whose name I changed. Every time you call her name Abraham, you will be reminded of how much I treasure your wife. You will know how highly she is regarded by the Most High God. Every time you call her by her name, it will establish in you a new regard for her as well.

Sarah had received a new name attached to a new future. Sarah did not say a word and The Most High, Almighty God had taken it upon himself to speak to her husband, changed her name and instructed her husband not to call her by the old name along with giving her the promise of a son and a due date! Verse 22 states that "God left off speaking with him and God went up from Abraham." God had spoken and advocated for Sarah.

Do you need God to advocate for you?

Become Sarah's daughter.

Do you need God to take your situation into His capable hands?

Become Sarah's daughter.

Do you need him to speak to your husband?

Become Sarah's daughter.

Do you desire a different future?

Join the movement and become Sarah's daughter.

You may be saying, Dawne, God's moved for me before and I've messed up. I've gotten myself in another relationship or marriage and I don't think God will do that for me again. Become Sarah's daughter. God changed her name and promised her a son. Note how the Lord showed up in Chapter 18:10, "And He said I will certainly return to you according to the time of life and lo, Sarah, your wife shall have a son." Note that this was the first time that Sarah heard God speaking about her with her own ears and she followed her husband's response, Sarah laughed! Even with this, God still kept His word and gave Sarah the desire of her heart! For those of you that think "I've messed up too much", become Sarah's daughter. Let God advocate for you. Let The Almighty God change your future and your marriage. Become Sarah's daughter.

You may be saying, Dawne, God fought for Sarah and brought her out of Pharaoh's house but my husband is the type that would have put me in Pharaoh's house more than once even after he saw God's deliverance. Guess what? Sarah's husband did too! What did I say? I said Sarah's husband did too! I couldn't believe it either but it's true. Genesis 20:1-2, confirms the story. "And" there's that word again. "And Abraham journeyed from there toward the South country, and dwelled between Kadesh and Shur and sojourned in Gerar. And Abraham said of Sarah, his wife, "She is my sister:" I thought... Didn't I just read this? When I realized it was a different situation I said, "Abraham, are you kidding me?"... "And Abimelech, King of Gerar sent and took Sarah." (Gen. 20:2) Look at the next word "But", But God. When we were little we used to say don't "but" into my business... but that's exactly what God did! God steps in right after one name is mentioned, "Sarah!!! "But God came to Abimelech in a dream by night, and said to him, "Behold you are but a dead man." ... Wait do you hear God's tone? God is seriously threatening to take this man's life because of Sarah! "for the woman which you have taken; for she is a man's wife." (Gen. 20:3)

But Abimelech had not come near her: and said Lord, will you slay also a righteous nation? Said he not to me, "She is my sister?" And she, even she herself said, "He is my brother: in the integrity of my heart and innocence of my hand have I done this." And God said to him in a dream, yea I know that you did this in the integrity of your heart, for I also withheld you from sinning against Me: therefore, I allowed you not to touch her. Now therefore, restore the man his wife; for he is a prophet and he shall pray for you, and you shall live: and if you restore her not; know that you shall surely die, and all that are yours." (Gen. 20: 4-7) Not only is God willing to kill this man because of Sarah but God is willing to kill this man and all that he has! Sarah has become God's prized possession and her obedience to her husband even when it places her in harm's way has become the key. God steps in for Sarah because of Sarah's commitment to respecting God's Kingdom order.

You may be asking if God will do this for you; here's the answer. Become Sarah's daughter and you will see God move for you like He has moved for Sarah, your spiritual mother... Is there more? Yes... "Therefore, Abimelech rose early in the morning,". . .(I bet he did, side note, I couldn't resist)... "And called all his servants, and told all these things in their ears: and the men were "sore" or greatly afraid. Then Abimelech called Abraham and said to him, what have you done to us? What have I offended you that you brought on me and on my Kingdom a great sin? You have done deeds to

146

me that ought not to be done. And Abimelech said to Abraham, "What saw you that you have done this thing?" And Abraham said because I thought surely the fear of God is not in this place; and they shall slay me for my wife's sake. And yet indeed she is my sister; she is the daughter of my father but not the daughter of my mother; and she became my wife. And it came to pass, when God caused us to wonder from my father's house, that I said to her, "This is your kindness which you shall show to me; at every place where we shall come, say of me, He is my brother." And Abimelech took sheep, and oxen and menservants and woman- servants, and gave and restored him Sarah his wife. And Abimelech said, behold, my land is before you; dwell where it pleases you. To Sarah he said, behold I have given your brother a thousand pieces of silver: behold he is to you a covering of the eyes to all that are with you, and with all other: thus, she was reproved. So, Abraham prayed to God: and God healed Abimelech, and his wife, and his maidservants, and they bore children. For the Lord had fast closed up all the wombs of the house of Abimelech, because of Sarah, Abraham's wife". (Gen. 20: 8-18)

Abraham put Sarah in harm's way not just once. Even though Abraham saw the delivery of Sarah out of Pharaoh's house, Abraham did exactly the same thing - again! Yes, "And", God showed up to protect Sarah again! Even though God used a dream as His means of communication and visitation God still showed up because of Sarah and for Sarah. God showed compassion in His warning to Abimelech. God not only reasoned with him when Abimelech pleaded for his life, God states that He, God, The Almighty, kept Abimelech from touching Sarah! God then gives instruction to Abimelech to return Sarah and have her husband pray for him. God follows with the consequences; if you do what I say, you will live. If you do not return Sarah you will die. God tops it off with... "and all that are yours." God is merciful even in his correction.

So once more, Abraham does not protect Sarah, so The Most High God shows up immediately to protect her because Sarah respected and honored Kingdom order. Sarah obeyed Abraham and God covered her. It is important to know that this time God is not sending plagues, God has gone straight to death! Sarai is not in danger this time, it is Sarah, the mother of nations. Sarah's future has been promised and God is not going to allow anyone to destroy it. Some of you may be saying that Sarah is different from you but let me remind you that Sarah had a husband that made decisions that put her in harm's way. Sarah had a husband that put himself first. Sarah had a husband that had flaws, yet he was a man of God. Sarah had a husband that made mistakes. Sarah had a husband that she had every reason not to follow yet Sarah chose to trust that if she remained in obedience, God would deliver her. Some of you may be saying Sarah probably wasn't there very long. Sarah probably was only taken for a few days. I wish that was true but verse 17 and 18 proves otherwise; "So Abraham prayed to God and God healed Abimelech and his wife, and his maidservants and they bore children for the Lord had fast closed up all the wombs of the house of Abimelech, because of Sarah, Abraham's wife"! (Gen. 20:17-18)

Take note in order for the women to notice that no one was getting pregnant or having babies, the period of gestation would have to pass. It suggests that Sarah had to have been taken for at least nine months. The most powerful 3 words are at the end. Gen. 20: 18: "Because of Sarah…."

Just think your name could be in her place. And God spoke to your husband because of _____. and God came to _____ in a dream by night because of _____.

God not only fought for Sarah but he visited Sarah. "And The Lord visited Sarah as He had said, and the Lord did to Sarah as He had spoken. For Sarah conceived and bore Abraham a son in his old age at this set time of which God had spoken to him." (Gen. 21:1-2) God gave Sarah the desire of her heart. Sarah was given a son. Sarah's dreams were fulfilled by God! Sarah finally had her 'happily ever after' and when someone upset it… The Almighty God stepped in! When Sarah had her son Isaac and Ishmael, Hagar's son mocked her, Sarah asked Abraham to send away Hagar and Ishmael! Harsh, don't you think? Abraham thought her request was unreasonable and had no intentions of saying yes but God showed up again and spoke to Abraham telling him "in all that Sarah has said to you, hearken to her voice;" (Gen. 21:12)

Can you imagine The Most High God, The Almighty, showing up and speaking to your husband saying, "In all that _____ has said to you hearkened to her voice;" that is the power of being Sarah's daughter…God fights personally for you!

Once you stay in Kingdom order, God will get in your business too! When I read, "Even as Sarah obeyed Abraham, calling him lord: whose daughters you are, as long as you do well, and are not afraid with any amazement." (1Peter 3:6) I thought "obeyed" isn't had a bit "strong"? But after diving into the life of Sarah I have come to see that there is such power in being Sarah's daughter that I have no problem with the "obey". Sarah got everything that she desired and more. Sarah caught the attention of the Most High God. Sarah was the only woman in the Bible whose name was changed by God. Pharaoh's house was plagued greatly because of Sarah. Abimelech was almost killed because of Sarah. God shut up the wombs of all of the women in Abimelech's house because of Sarah. God came in a dream to Abimelech because of Sarah. God sent an angel to tell Hagar to return her mistress to because of Sarah. The Lord visited Sarah and created a miracle for her to have a son at an old age because

He valued Sarah. God stepped in and spoke to Abraham because of Sarah. God told Abraham to send Hagar and Ishmael away because of Sarah. Becoming Sarah's daughter changed my marriage and my life.

I watched God give me everything I desired as I laid down my will, like Sarah,- and stayed in Kingdom order. God stepped in for me and gave me my 'happily ever after' when I became Sarah's daughter.

MY TESTIMONY

Allow me bring it home. When my husband and I decided to get married I wanted us to buy a new house. I did not want to live in the house where he lived. When I brought the subject up to him, he was unyielding. He explained that he loved his house and he was not moving. He explained that he loved the neighborhood and he was not moving. Each time I brought up the subject it led to a disagreement. My husband finally called me one day and said that if I wanted him to move out of that house when we got married it was a "deal breaker" for him and we should not get married!!

I was shocked! I prayed and God was clear that I should move in. I did once we were married but I was unhappy in my spirit about being there. I began making changes to the house. I painted and began to redecorate and God began to direct me to Sarah. I began to study the concept and I reluctantly embraced it. I was so accustomed to having to fight for what I wanted my entire life. The concept with someone else really fighting for me was foreign. My husband was a generous man and we spoiled each other but this was a big deal to me and I was getting frustrated. The Lord told me to become Sarah's daughter. He told me not to ask my husband for anything. He told me anything I wanted, I was to ask Him, God. He explained Kingdom order to me and told me that He was head of our house, then my husband, then myself, then the children. He told me to be in total respect of my husband and his position. He reinforced the fact that men need respect and that love cannot replace respect for them. He explained that I can trust His headship and He would make sure that He took care of me.

I listened. He explained that once I stayed in His Kingdom order He would cover me. He further explained that if I asked Him for something and my husband said no and it was something that He saw that I desired that lined up with his plan, He would bring it about. I began to pray about being Sarah's Daughter. I began to study Sarah. God then told me that He wanted me to write a book about it but I'd have to "live it first". I began to live and breathe whatever I could read about Sarah. I began to see God moving in my marriage like never before.

I kept my mouth shut at times when my flesh just wanted to open it. That was the most difficult part and it seemed like I prayed constantly. Then I was told to pray in the middle of the night. I was told to ask the Holy Ghost to wake me up in the middle of the night when my husband was most susceptible to the function of the Holy Ghost in his subconscious and I was told to lift up my hands over him and pray. I decided that I would do just that. The first night when I prayed that the Holy Ghost would wake me up in the middle of the night, I forgot that I asked and I found myself sitting straight up and wide-awake! It took me a second to realize what was going on. I raised my hands over my husband and I began to pray. I prayed blessings over him and I prayed that anything that God wanted to give me would come through my husband. I prayed until I fell asleep. I was awakened and prayed every night for nine nights. On the morning of the ninth night my husband called me. I was visiting with a girlfriend at home. He said "write this down". It was an address and he said get there as quickly as possible. I left immediately. My girlfriend rode with me. I had no idea what was happening. I pulled up to a big beautiful house at the end of a cul-de-sac. I left my girlfriend in the car and walked up to the front door and rang the doorbell. To my surprise, my husband opened the door and said, "This is going to be our house and both of our names will be on it." The following day he placed an offer on the house. In 10 days God did what I've been trying to accomplish for what seemed like forever! I became Sarah's Daughter and The Most High God stepped in to work for me. God showed me that only He, not Disney, can take me to the "Real Happily Ever After"

Follow the steps to become Sarah's daughter and watch God do the same for you!

Declaration NOT to Play the Chess or Checker Game with My Marriage.

How to know if you've been playing the chess or checker game:

If you were going to do something for your husband and you change your mind based on his actions, something he did or did not do, you're playing the chess or checker game.

If he does something hurtful and you focus on making sure you hurt him in return,

you're playing the chess or checkers game.

If he drops the ball and you know it was not deliberate and you seek to, "drop the ball" as well, "sort of accidentally", you're playing the chess or checkers game.

If you are using "anyone or anything" to make him jealous, you're playing the chess or checker game.

If you are doing anything to call forth a "reaction" other than his natural behavior or response, you're playing the chess or checker game.

If you see an opportunity to take advantage of him in anyway and you move forward with it like a checkers game where you would jump on the board several times because they did not see the move, you're playing chess or checkers with your marriage.

If you operate in any manner where you are manipulating or trying to control him, you're playing chess or checkers with your marriage.

I commit NOT to play chess or checkers with my marriage and my future.

Signature_____

Date_____

Decree and Declare

Father, I accept Your Kingdom Order. Father, I make you Head of my home and my life. Father, I commit to You as the head. My husband as next in command and I come under. I trust you to fight for me and I commit to being "I AM Sarah's Daughter." Cover our family in Jesus name.

I, _____ commit to becoming "I AM Sarah's Daughter." I commit my family under the headship and authority of God through Jesus Christ. I recognize the kingdom order as:

God

My husband, _____

Wife _____

I commit to becoming "I AM Sarah's Daughter" I claim all the benefits in Jesus name.

_____

_____

I commit to sharing the power of "I AM Sarah's Daughter" with others.

_____

_____

Signature   Date

I commit to attend an, "I AM Sarah's Daughters" conference.

_____

_____

Signature   Date

Additional Resources:

Want More Change in Your Marriage? Go Deeper:

Get

"I Am Sarah's Daughter..-The Workbook

Additional books by Dawne Kirkwood-Santi

"I AM Sarah's Daughter How To Get God's Attention in Your Marriage.. The Real Happily Ever After –The Workbook": Powerful!

This workbook is created to take the reader into a deeper personal discovery for supernatural breakthrough using thought provoking questions and exercises. This workbook journal is perfect for individuals, book clubs, bridal parties, women's retreats, women's conferences, professional marriage counseling resource, women's trainings and breakout sessions. Used with prayer expect supernatural breakthroughs.

"Giving Birth to Me; The Guide to Success in Birthing Your Dreams"

"Giving Birth To Me" is a self-help empowerment book given to Dawne through the power of The Holy Ghost. The analogy of birthing is used in an impactful- life changing manner to prompt success and positive change. Women have used this book successfully to lose weight, end toxic relationships, create loving relationships, continue their education, start businesses and other upward movements including self-care. This book comes with a journal workbook in the back to bring about even greater accountability. The author can be contacted to purchase "Giving Birth to Me" while supplies last as presently Amazon is sold out of new copies. Free Bookmarks are provided while supplies last. The author can be messaged through Facebook, Instagram or Twitter.

Subscribe www.IAMSarahsdaughter.com

Have Dawne Kirkwood-Santi speak at your next event.

Contact us: IAMSarahsdaughter@gmail.com

Follow the Author @dawnekirkwoodsanti

Message the author on Facebook or Instagram.

Reflection Questions

Is it possible that Sarah was blaming herself for God's silence?

_____

_____

_____-

Has God ever seemed silent and you felt like it was your fault?

_____

_____

How has this book helped you?

_____

Are there women in your life that you believe would benefit from this book? List them:

_____

_____

_____

_____

Invite them to read it and become, "I AM Sarah's Daughter"

I invited ___ many women to read the book and Join the Movement.

God has promised that through Abram and Sarai "all families of the earth shall be blessed" (Gen.12:3)

Bless a family…give this book as a gift! Bless a family ..share this book with family and friends!